T0354971

God COMES TO Man In Jesus

DR. JOHN THOMAS WYLIE

authorHOUSE

AuthorHouse™
1663 Liberty Drive
Bloomington, IN 47403
www.authorhouse.com
Phone: 1 (800) 839-8640

Published by AuthorHouse 12/13/2019

ISBN: 978-1-7283-3973-3 (sc)
ISBN: 978-1-7283-3972-6 (e)

Print information available on the last page.

This book is printed on acid-free paper.

Contents

Introduction

"When The Time Had Fully Come"

"When the time had fully come, God sent forth his Son," the messenger Paul clarified (Gal. 4:4 NIV). In the following few lessons we will examine in detail how God did this. As we approach Christmas, 2019, these lessons will assist us with focusing on the focal reality of God's intervention in mankind's history in the person of Jesus Christ.

Maybe the story has turned out to be standard for a few; maybe some have lost the effect of what it implied for God to give his only beloved Son to the world, to send his beloved to be crucified for the sins of the world.

Be that as it may, this sort of good news is everlastingly new; it doesn't become stale. The explanation is that in all times and in all places there are people who need to experience the marvel, the wonder of God's love in their own lives.

These people occupy our churches, as well. The people who come to worship are not free of personal needs and issues. They come to seek Jesus Christ since they need a touch of the powerful, the supernatural in their lives.

People come with hope and assurance since they know God cares. If God couldn't have cared less about them, we never would observe Christmas. This coming month of December will find people still engaged with a spin of social activities and church activities, but these must not be allowed to darken the truth, or the reality of God's care. People are hurting today from physical, social, and emotional needs, and Christians have the wonderful news to share about God's love in Jesus Christ.

These lessons should compel us to reconsider our own needs, to pose inquiries about spiritual lack of interest and hardness even with God's compassion on lost humankind, and to search for those who need the consolation and hope that Jesus Christ's coming brings to the table. Faith and assurance are built on the realities of the Christmas event, not on a mindless holiday celebration.

Chapter One

The Angel's Mission
(Luke 1:26-28)

LUKE ALONE RECORDS THE details of the angel's mission to Mary. Matthew advises how a blessed messenger(angel) revealed to Joseph that he ought not separate (divorce) from Mary (Matt. 1:18-21 KJV). Neither Mark nor John give any insights regarding Christ's introduction (His birth) to the world. In these verses we have the area of this dramatic scene and the recognizable proof of those chosen by God to be the earthly parents of his beloved Son.

Gabriel Was Sent By God
(v. 26)

The timing of Gabriel's mission is according to by the length of Elizabeth's pregnancy: "in the 6th month." Elizabeth was to be the mother of John the Baptist, the forerunner, or announcer, of Messiah's coming. He was "to prepare for the Lord a people prepared" (1:17).

Gabriel's mission originated with God the Father. God sent his emissary to make known his plan. God didn't hide from the people involved what he was about to do. God speaks with his people; the Bible is one long discussion, in a manner of speaking, among God and the people he made to have personal fellowship with himself.

So the celestial dispatcher (the divine messenger, an angel) went to a particular town, Nazareth. God was going to achieve the most marvelous wonder ever, and there must be a fitting declaration. Everything considered, we may expect that God would have accomplished something that would have pulled in the consideration of the whole world immediately (as he will do when Jesus returns once more).

In any case, at the Savior's first appearance the principal declaration was to be a private undertaking. God sent Gabriel: that was sufficient to indicate he loved and cared about Mary and Joseph.

Gabriel Was Sent To The Virgin Mary
(vv. 27, 28)

The holy messenger (angel) was sent to a young woman living in Nazareth. Her name was Mary

Dr. John Thomas Wylie

and she was engaged to wed Joseph. Joseph had a place not just with the equivalent hereditary branch from which David was descended, yet explicitly to the house which had David as its founder.

The Savior himself was to be of David's line (cf. v. 32). As the adopted child of Joseph, Jesus was legitimately a relative of David. A few researchers imagine that Mary was likewise of the immediate heredity of David, in spite of the fact that the gospel scholars in no place express this to be so. The central matter of Matthew 1:20, Luke 1:27 and 2:4 is to be presented the Davidic plummet of Christ. The tribes of Israel were partitioned into families, and the families into "houses."

The critical reality about Mary is that she was a virgin (cf. Matt. 1:23, 25). We know nothing of her family foundation or her age, despite the fact that it has by and large been assumed that she was still in her teens. We will note below something of her imperative faith and commitment to God.

Despite the fact that she had neither distinction (fame) nor notoriety (reputation) now, and in spite of the fact that the Bible gives no proof concerning why God chose her to be the mother of his beloved Son, we are sure that she was a devout, godly person.

Until the late nineteenth century, the virgin birth of Christ was an unchallenged article of the Christian faith. The appearance of the scientific age brought a spirit hostile to anti-supernaturalism, with the goal that this wonder and the others in the Bible were discounted.

Also, a few researchers said virgin birth stories were actually part of antiquated folklore, and early Christians just concocted one of their own. Others called attention to the doctrinal parts of the New Testament don't make reference to the virgin birth.

Nonetheless, the righteousness of God's Son is an innate necessity of his deity and the reality of New Testament doctrine is precisely that the one who knew no transgression (sin) removed the condemnation of sinners (II Cor. 5:21; I Pet. 3:18). The Bible teaches the transmission of sin nature from one generation to the next (Rom. 5:12), with the goal that everyone is born into the world a sinner.

Clearly, at that point, God's Son, if he somehow to be sinless, would have to be born into the world some other way. As Luke 1:35 shows,

Dr. John Thomas Wylie

the child was "holy, the Son of God" since he had no human father, but was conceived by the Holy Spirit.

That Mary didn't remain a virgin for her entire life is shown by Matthew 1:25 and Luke 2:7 ("first-born son"). Afterward, we meet the brothers and sisters of Jesus, consistently in connection with Mary (Matt. 12:46; 13:54-56; John 2:12; Acts 1:14).

The angel addressed Mary as God's "favored one." the same word is used in Ephesians 1:6 in reference to God's grace being "freely bestowed" on believers. The choice of Mary was the all of God's grace, just as salvation itself is. Mary didn't earn the honor, she was simply blessed by God's choice of her (cf. v. 42).

The significant actuality isn't how or why she was favored, but the fact that God was with her. The faithful, godly Jews held God at a manageable distance in reverential awe and dread; they were not used to the idea of a close personal revelation of God.

In fact, those who experienced angels and other heavenly appearances (divine manifestations) thought they would terminate on the spot (cf. Judges 13:22). God, obviously, was "with" Mary in the general way he is with all believers, but this announcement of Gabriel's was to make ready (pave the way) for an extraordinary, special relationship.

(What do you find out about what God is like from these verses? What confidence does this give you about God today? How does he deliver his messages to people today? For what reason do you figure the scriptural writers don't reveal more realities about the background of Joseph and Mary? Would you be interested in knowing more about them? Why?)

The Angel's Message
(Luke 1:29-33 KJV)

The rest of this unusual experience comprises of a discussion among Gabriel and Mary. The angel previously reported that Mary would bring forth God's Son; at that point, in light of Mary's inquiry, he clarified how this would occur. Matthew tells how an angel visited Joseph after he discovered that his betrothed was pregnant. Luke takes us back a step prior and shows how Mary comprehended what would come to pass (what would transpire) before Joseph did.

Mary's Bewilderment
(v. 29)

The angel's appearance and welcome disturbed Mary. Luke shows that she was incredibly upset and bothered by this startling disclosure. The angel's response (v. 30) demonstrates that in addition to the fact that she was vexed she was afraid too.

However she held enough self-restraint to ponder what was occurring. Presumably she was thinking about what she had done, positive or negative, good or bad, to warrant a heavenly guest. No doubt she found the occasion troubling in light of her profoundly instilled hesitance to have such a personal experience with the living God.

However her faith and confidence were with the end goal that she didn't fall in terror. Maybe she was one of the many in Israel who were praying and yearning for God to visit his people.

She Would Bear A Son
(vv. 30, 31)

Gabriel initially comforted Mary and assured her again that she had d found favor with God. She was not going to be made a judged for any offenses. The reason for this celestial appearance was not to bring judgment, however to bring news that God chose to reveal himself in human form.

God's plan started with the choice of a human mother. Her child would be a son and she was to name him Jesus (Joshua in Hebrew), which means Savior. The words of the holy messenger (angel) in verse 31 deliberately conform with the language of Isaiah's well known prophecy (Isa. 7:14 KJV).

The extraordinary supernatural occurrence (the great miracle) of the manifestation was going to be unfolded (cf. Heb. 1:2). God was taking a straightforward (simple) human instrument; he was coming to earth through the procedure of human birth. The Savior was to be like us in each respect, yet without sin (Heb. 4:15 KJV).

The pre-incarnate, eternal Word (John 1:1, 2) was to become temporal; God the Son was to become the Son of man, Jesus of Nazareth. His humanity was completely insisted (affirmed) by the name he chose for himself: eighty-one times Jesus called himself the Son of man. By this name he distinguishes the two forms of his existence. With this self-designation he confesses himself as the Son of God come in the flesh.

Her son Will Be God's Son
(vv. 32, 33)

Gabriel's further disclosure is a powerful reverberation of Isaiah 9:6, 7 and II Samuel 7:12-14. His words depict the significance of Mary's son as the Jewish Messiah, or anointed king in the line of David who would rule over an everlasting kingdom. Her child would genuinely be the Son of God.

These words captured the highest standard (expectation) of the godly Jews (cf. Luke 2:25). David's throne was what they ached to see restored. "The house of Jacob" represented his physical descendants, the Jews. Gabriel took these expectations, condensed them, and made them throb with the excitement of coming glory.

Here was the first inkling that God was going to end 400 years of his silence since he had last spoken through the prophets.

The main impact here is that Messiah will be a powerful figure whose authority will rest on his divine origin. In his coming he will claim the rightful prerogatives of deity. He will be more than an earthly potentate, because he "will be called the Son of the Most High."

Later on, when he claimed at his preliminary to be the Son of God, he was rejected, denounced for sacrilege (blasphemy), and crucified (cf. Mark 14:62, 63; Luke 22:66-71; Matt. 26:64-66). This was to be the focal issue of personal and corporate decision about him: Was he truly God manifest in human flesh? Did he truly originate from the Father?

In his prayer the evening of his betrayal, Jesus was appreciative that his supporters had faith in his divinity: "They have accepted that thou didst send me...these know that thou hast sent me" (John 17:8, 25 RSV).

Today this continues being the focal point of Christian conviction. The church follows more than an extraordinary religious teacher; the church is headed by God the Son. True, he came as the Son of man with full humanity, but his full divinity (deity) makes his past, present, and future work for believers effective. If he were not completely God, then his payment of the death penalty on the cross would not be fully effective.

Having come as the Son of man, the Lord Jesus after the cross returned to the Father. The church praises him and honors him now as the Son of God; at some future point he again will

Dr. John Thomas Wylie

be perceived by all the world as the Son of man (Luke 21:27 NIV).

Gabriel's declaration in this way envelops the ultimate mystery of the Christian faith: How could Mary's son be God's Son? The Bible doesn't reply, but to state that Jesus - although living with the Father in heaven, "as God" - actually "emptied himself" and was "born in the likeness of men" (Phil. 2:6, 7 RSV).

Ever since the apostle Paul composed those words, scholars (theologians) have grappled with the humanly impossible question of how the divine - human Jesus (the God-Man) could be united in one person. Gabriel didn't tell Mary, and God doesn't disclose to us now. It is a conviction of personal faith in the truth of Scripture.

(How might Gabriel's portrayal of the infant's destiny support Mary? For what reason would it say it was significant for Gabriel to outline his declaration in the wording of the Old Testament predictions? What encouragement and inspiration do you get from this declaration? Does it mean anything else to you today than it would have to Mary? Why? What do you know today that Mary didn't know then? Why is the full deity of Jesus Christ still a stumblingblock to some people today? How would you respond to the people who don't accept this truth?)

The Angel's Explanation
(Luke 1:34-38 KJV)

The humanly unimaginable is conceivable (human impossibilities is possible) with God. That is the Christian response to some supposed scholarly issues and logical inconsistencies. Mary had a similar issue in her mind, and the Lord graciously gave her an answer through the angel.

The angel didn't give moment details, but he forced Mary to think about the greatness of God's power. That is our refuge as well today. Christians believe in a God of the impossible.

Mary's Confusion
(v. 34)

Mary didn't contest the realities of the heavenly attendant's (the angel's) message: she didn't question that what he had declared would in fact happened, but she needed to know how it would occur. Her inquiry was straightforward: How can the laws of physical birth be broken? Since her heart was in the perfect spot, she was granted an answer. Mary's inquiry, obviously, reveals that she was thinking about an immediate conception, not of conception following her marriage. She had a husband as in the sense she was locked in (engaged) to Joseph, but in those days generally a year passed between engagement and marriage.

She Would Conceive By The Holy Spirit's Power
(v. 35)

The angel's answer clarified that Mary's son was not to be a earthly Messiah, only adopted by God as his Son. His birth into the world would be because of the power of the Holy Spirit coming upon her so that her child would be "holy," i.e., divine. The essential importance of "holy" is "separated to God," so it can mean divine.

The Spirit's coming upon Mary is depicted in language like that portraying the resting of the glory of God on the Old Testament tabernacle (cf. Exod. 40:35). "The power of the Most High" is the immediate energy of the godhead passed on by the Holy Spirit. The result of this baffling work (mysterious work) of God is a child who is to be "the Son of God."

In this way, at last, we are left with mystery; we can only say what the Bible itself says: the virgin birth of Christ was the result of supernatural action in a human vessel. The infant was not two sons - Mary's and the Father's - however one. The Bible insists this basic solidarity but connects Christ's human birth with his legitimate (proper) relationship to God.

God Had Already Done The Impossible For Elizabeth (vv. 36, 37)

In confirmation of his word the angel spoke about the miracle previously experienced by Elizabeth, Mary's relative. This was a miracle in light of the fact that both Elizabeth and her better half were "advanced in years" (v. 18) and Elizabeth was barren (v. 7).

Mary without a doubt was familiar with Elizabeth's case, so the news that she was pregnant would be accepted as a sign of God's intervention. Mary didn't demand a sign, but the Lord granted her one in anyway.

Gabriel expressed the same truth that was revealed to Sarah when she limited the likelihood that she could have a baby (cf. Gen. 18:14 KJV). On this statement Mary's faith had to rest. It had to do with the boundless power of God, not with how he would achieve the birth of His Son, but simply that he would do it in defiance of the typical human, physical laws.

God himself has built up those physical laws of procreation, however for this situation because his Son was to be fully divine and sinless, those laws would be set aside. Mary had to rest in the conviction that God could do that.

Mary's Submission
(v. 38)

Mary quietly accepted her high honor. Here is great, marvelous faith in such conditions. Mary was no unconscious robot in carrying out God's plan, but with humility and faith she considered herself to be a fellow-worker with the purpose of God.

In this way, she had to give her own consent to his plan and purpose. Hers is a lovely proclamation of submission to God's will. In this kind of submission to God's word every Christian finds the most profound fulfillment and satisfaction.

But our faith must be challenged as Mary's was. Could you be accept the announcement the of the impossible? When we confide in God in the face of obstacles or hindrances, we find the true meaning of submission.

(What choices did Mary have? For what reason do you think she obeyed in faith? What impossibilities do you have to trust God for?)

The account of every divine - human experience is exciting and inspiring. God acts today to draw his plan to our attention. He gives adequate proof for a response of faith and obedience. We can't demand signs from angels since God has spoken in his Son, the Word made flesh, and in his written Word. God has every right to expect us to repent and obey the gospel.

Chapter Two

The Coming Anticipated
(Luke 1:39-55 KJV)

EVERY AGE HAS ITS political pioneers who report that better days are coming. This promise is continually held before people. Grown-ups are advised to buckle down and bolster the administration's projects on account of the sort of life we need to work for our children later on. People are encouraged and they feed on the expectation that by one way or another around the curve there will be a superior arrangement/plan for all.

Ponder what you envision. Is it not some slight help from obligation, from the weight of bringing home the bacon, from the strain of living with some disease, from the vulnerability about youngsters, friends and family, and companions? The majority of us would envision a real existence free from wrongdoing, from war, from destitution, from lack of education, from liquor abuse, etc.

However for a great many people this kind of expectation is attached to human inventiveness. Maybe somebody will discover a remedy for malignant growth. Maybe we will have the option to have an arrangement of anticipation and justice that will control wrongdoing. Maybe somebody will concoct a contamination free vehicle motor that keeps running on less fuel.

Many find in these human goals their sole reason for living. Political leaders, labor leaders, teachers, and agents realize they need to characterize their objectives in wording that will fulfill these human expectations. In any case, what does the church need to say? What expectation does the church bring to the table? Do Christians have any desires that are unique?

There is one single string of expectation (hope) that sustains the Christian: Jesus Christ. Before his coming faithful people shivered with expectation of his coming. Presently we know that he has come to save us. The inquiry this Christmas is whether or not we see Christ the only possible, and conceivable fulfillment of human aspirations.

Do we foresee him as the solution to our most profound needs? People are dying without expectation even at Christmas since they know nothing personal about Christ.

In this lesson we will consider the excitement that grasped Mary and Elizabeth fully expecting Christ's coming. His world ought to propel us today to look for him with new expectation (hope) about how he can come into our lives, change us, and fulfill us.

Elizabeth's Blessing Of Mary
(Luke 1:39-45 KJV)

The events of this lesson following those of the past lesson. Mary had heard the heavenly angel Gabriel's announcement and she had responded in faith and obedience.

The angel had disclosed to her that Elizabeth was pregnant regardless of her old age. What pursues is one of the most delicate but then exciting scenes in the Bible; the common rejoicing and support (encouragement) between two of God's most favored people. The explanation behind their excitement is that God was going to accomplish something sensational, dramatic; he was going to come to earth in human form.

We don't have know when when Mary chose to visit her relative Elizabeth, yet the general impression is that it wasn't long after Gabriel's declaration. Actually, Luke says she "went with haste," which recommends that Mary could barely wait to impart the news to another person.

You can envision how she more likely than not felt right now. Be that as it may, the inquiry would be, Who might she be able to tell about the angel's appearance? Maybe her own family. She was not yet married and living with Joseph, yet nothing is said about her parents and brothers and sisters. Maybe it would have appeared to be pompous to let them know.

Elizabeth was the sensible one since she was a relative (tradition says a cousin, yet the word doesn't show such a near relationship) and furthermore on the grounds that she figured in Gabriel's declaration.

In the event that Elizabeth's pregnancy were surely a sign that God would intervene and send Messiah into the world, at that point she ought to be the first to know the following stage in God's plan.

Elizabeth's child would prepare the hearts of the people to receive Mary's child.

Mary's was not a concise social call. She stayed three months with Elizabeth (cf. v. 56), and what is recorded in our lesson is their first meeting. Mary headed out from Nazareth to an anonymous (unnamed) city in Judah, the area immediately around Jerusalem toward the south of Galilee.

Elizabeth's husband Zechariah, a priest in Jerusalem, was presently at home (v. 23), having been struck dumb in light of the fact that he didn't accept the angel's prophecy (v. 20).

He could hear what Mary and Elizabeth were saying, but he couldn't go into their discussion. How disappointing and frustrating that more likely than not been for him at this exciting time. Afterward, after his wife brought forth John (gave birth to John), Zechariah's tongue was loosed and he praised God.

Elizabeth Was Filled With The Holy Spirit
(v. 41)

Luke doesn't let us know explicitly what Mary said to Elizabeth, only that she welcomed her. Clearly, be that as it may, her welcome was more than "hi." Her greeting without a doubt was the announcement of what Gabriel had advised her. We assemble this from Elizabeth's reaction.

Her first response was physical; her very own child jumped in her belly. Elizabeth was a half year pregnant right now, and mothers know how children can kick, however this was something strange, and Elizabeth knew it (v. 44).

Her second response was spiritual, the filling of the Holy Spirit. God was giving his servant the joy of not only bearing Messiah's forerunner, but in addition the joy of blessing Messiah's mother. This was the unique, special work of the Holy Spirit on her behalf.

The Holy Spirit's role preceding his happening upon the church at Pentecost was to empower, enable godly people to carry out special ministries. Now at this point in history a special work was needed to confirm what God was about to do. In any event, something as basic as the meeting of these two women was blessed by an uncommon, but special visitation of the Holy Spirit.

Mary Is Bless Because Of God's Choice
(vv. 42, 43)

The Holy Spirit inspired Elizabeth to give a twofold blessing upon Mary and her child. The implication, obviously, is that her approval, her blessing is from God himself. Mary was not honored in light of the fact that she was immaculate; she was blessed in light of the fact that God chose her in sovereign mercy. Elizabeth's blessing is an affirmation of this reality. Elizabeth was not lifting up the human at the expense of the divine; she basically was commending the joyous ramifications for Mary.

She was overpowered and wanted Mary to know that she was for sure fortunate to be chosen from among all women of the earth to be the mother of Jesus Christ. This touching human dramatization shows how God's good news was received and loved and acknowledged as an invaluable gift (a priceless blessing). Elizabeth knew that Mary's child was above all and most importantly to be uniquely blessed because of its celestial (divine) conception.

This was the proper time for the Holy Spirit to fill God's divinely chosen ones with great joy and happiness. Elizabeth had walked with God for quite a long time (for years) (cf. 1:6) and her blessing originated from a heart that had longed for God's salvation. Now she was going to see it come to pass.

Yet she was properly humbled at the prospect. She confessed that Mary's unborn infant was her Lord and it was beyond her that Mary should come to invest time with her. The righteous walk in this mentality before God, not feeling that they merit or deserve his special blessings.

Elizabeth found in Mary's visit a gracious touch from the Lord. It was a marvelous privilege to have fellowship with the person who was to bear God's Son. This kind of humility, gratitude, and praise are the characteristics or marks of genuine faith.

Mary Is Blessed Because of Her Faith (vv. 44, 45)

Elizabeth Told Mary how her own infant jumped in her belly when she heard Mary's uplifting news. This was not just a characteristic reflex; something bizarre occurred, on the grounds that Elizabeth said her infant "jumped for joy."

In some way, John who was to prepare the path for Jesus, was moved to respond. Evidently, there is no normal clarification for this, yet Elizabeth and Mary accepting it as another confirmation from the Lord.

Elizabeth at that point favored Mary for her faith in God's promises. She herself had seen the opposite in her significant other's absence of faith (cf. 1:20). Mary's faith in the angel's words was seen not only in the manner she responded to Gabriel, but also in the manner in which she communicated his disclosure to Elizabeth.

There is no uncertainty that she certainly expected "a fulfillment of what was spoken to her from the Lord." Instead of faltering despite such a breathtaking improvement, she just trusted it and believed it could occur as Gabriel had said.

God in his leniency (mercy) was pleased to unite two women of no extraordinary human notoriety. They accepted his grace with humility and rejoiced in it. Their basic greeting has the ring of realness about it. The Lord Jesus was born among average folks, but people with an unmistakable (distinctive) handle of spiritual realities.

(What sentiments may Mary have had now in her life? Shouldn't something be said about Elizabeth? Do you think she was envisioning a further disclosure from the Lord? How is the value of a spiritual encounter enhanced by sharing with another person? How would you respond to the blessing of God in somebody's life? What was expected of both Mary and Elizabeth for this to be a Spirit-favored experience? How open do you feel toward God's really accomplishing for you what he has promised? Do you figure the Holy Spirit can use you to favor (bless) another person? How?)

Mary's Rejoicing In God
(Luke 1:46-55 KJV)

These expressions of praise by Mary in response to Elizabeth's benediction are known as the Magnificat (taken from the Latin for "it magnifies," the first word in the Greek and Latin content). Her glorious considerations have been combined with a good music and the melody is used particularly as a major aspect of vespers or evensong in some churches.

The focal theme is thanksgiving to God for his goodness to Mary and to his people. In thinking about Mary's expressions, one needs to recollect that her language is established in the imagery and promises of the Old Testament. It is filled with echoes of Old Testament acclaim, particularly from Hannah's psalm (I Sam. 2:1-10).

The wording comes out of this general Jewish frame of reference and isn't the explicitly Christian praise that came later. It is, in any case, a model of devotional praise to God.

God Himself Was The Object Of Mary's Joy (vv. 46,47)

Her heart was flooding in light of what God had accomplished for her. Such unrestrained praise is pleasing to God and is the characteristic of the people who love him and want to do his will.

This kind of praise can't be manufactured; it isn't standard; it's anything but a matter of religious exercise. Mary's song sprang from a heart that was profoundly moved. Only a heart that has been influenced by God's affection (love) can respond along these lines.

Her whole being was united in magnifying, or expanding, enlarging God. Whatever God accomplishes for us, if we respond in faith, the purpose for existing is to enable us to see God larger and larger in our lives.

Mary perceived her basic situation as a sinful person (a sinful human) before God. Along these lines, God must be her Savior. She knew she was not impeccable. She knew that salvation came only through God's grace and mercy. Had she not known God thusly, she would not have been spiritually prepared to be the mother of Jesus.

All that she had from God was a result of her seeing who she was before a holy God. Accordingly, during this time of uncommon appearance (special visitation) she could rejoice with unadulterated euphoria (pure joy). Her joy right now was in God, not in the child; in the Giver; not in the gift. This was simply the joy of anticipation and faith.

Mary Rejoiced In What God Had Done For Her Personally (vv. 48-50)

Now we have the explanations behind Mary's song of commendation (praises). She pronounces that God "has respected the low estate of his handmaiden" and God "has accomplished extraordinary things for me." What was Mary's gauge of herself? We have noticed that she perceived her need for God to be her Savior.

In reacting to Gabriel, she said she was the Lord's handmaid (1:38). Now she uses that articulation once more. The essential idea is to be God's servant, to be heavily influenced by him (controlled by him), to pursue his will and not her own.

Her humility radiates through again in the articulation "low estate." This implies truly "humiliation." It demonstrate Mary's profound inclination of unworthiness for her signal honor. She was not saying thanks to God for how great she was. She basically was stunned that God would much consider using an individual such as herself.

However, in God's wonderful plan this humble young lady would one day be honored by "all ages." Why? Essentially in light of the fact that God had accomplished something great for her, not on the grounds that she was great in herself. Mary's blessing grows out of God's loving choice and her obedient faith. The two went inseparably (hand in hand).

God chose her, he accomplished something extraordinary, yet he didn't dismiss the personal element. Mary heard his call and obeyed. She was open to this most unusual act of God in mankind's history. She has the right to be perceived by all Christians as the beneficiary of God's blessing. However she herself, as this song appears, would coordinate praise and worship away from herself and toward God himself.

God's name is holy, Mary sings, and no person can claim that holiness in himself. The implication is that God came down to visit mankind - the God who is mighty and blessed gone as far as do this. Mary had such regard for God's power and holiness that she was overwhelmed that he would act on behalf the of such a humble, lowly person as she.

Our commendation should in like manner grow in the same soil. If we don't consider God to be mighty and holy, and if we are not amazed that he should enter into our lives, we will not be praise to praise him.

Mary's frame of mind toward God up to this point has been that of a rejoicing servant. Now she uses "fear" to describe a proper reverence for God (v. 50). This demeanor is major to a legitimate comprehension of one's walk before God. Mary isn't groveling in wretched dread; she is loaded with joy. In any case, Mary saw that to experience God's mercy whenever, one must walk before him with respect for his strength (his might) and holiness.

This mentality (attitude) is enjoined upon all believers. "Let us offer to God acceptable worship, with reverence and awe; for our God is a consuming fire" (Heb. 12:28, 29). Mary's song is a delightful, and beautiful example of "acceptable worship." We would do well to follow her example.

Mary Rejoiced In The Nature Of God's Work Among Men (vv. 51-53)

The God who is mighty doesn't conceal his strength from men. He reveals his power in many ways. Mary now envisions what God will do through Messiah. She looks to the past as the reason for what God will do later on. Every age of believers can anticipate that God to do likewise.

In these verses, Mary confirms that God scatters the proud, puts down the relentless (mighty), lifts up the modest (exalts the humble), fills the hungry, and sends the rich away empty-handed. These realities about God are colossal promises and warnings. There is no uncertainty from reading this what God searches for to bless and to chastise.

Human pride is a cursed thing (abomination) to the Lord. Those who are powerful (mighty) in human terms face horrendous reprisal from the Lord. Pride isn't confined to the powerful, but human political and military power become the most evident instances of human pride. Mary could review those occasions in the past when God had done this. The Old Testament contains numerous models, Nebuchadnezzar and Belshazzar among them.

The explanation behind God's action against the proud and the mighty is on the grounds that they won't recognize or acknowledge him as supreme. The issue in everybody's life is straightforward: Who will be the chief? Pride drives us to make ourselves chief. In the event that we do that, we incur God's righteous displeasure.

Then again, there is incredible encouragement here for the feeble, the humble, and the hungry - the poor of this world as embodied by Mary. You can envision her heavenly giggling now. God had not sent Jesus into the home of a well off, persuasive, esteemed Jewish religious leader.

Quite the opposite. God sent his Son into the home of a country peasant girl, a person of "low degree," poor and hungry in this current world's assets. In any case, how God had "filled" her and exalted her. This was another case of how God functioned totally in opposition to human desires and expectations. However, Mary saw the spiritual truth and praised God for it.

Mary Rejoiced In His Faithfulness To Israel (vv. 54, 55)

Mary returned to her Old Testament prophecy. She clearly knew God's word quite well. She now observed the fulfillment of God's promises to Abraham, to the fathers of Israel, and to Abraham's seed. For at least four centuries these promises appeared nil. Nothing was occurring.

It took incredible faith to claim them. Now Mary expresses gratitude toward God for remembering his leniency (mercy) to Israel. These people were to be the human stock of the Lord

Jesus Christ. His coming was connected to what God had said long ago in the past. So Mary is thankful for God's faithfulness to his word. The faith of God's people had been tested, but the people who shared Mary's faith were not to be frustrated, nor disappointed.

(From what you have seen of Mary here, would she be the sort of individual you would have been the mother of Jesus? Why or why not? OK, want her to be your mother? Your neighbor? How might you be like her her yourself?)

What's your opinion of when you consider Mary? A woman in an old painting with a radiance sparkling (halo) over her head? Mary was a real individual with genuine sentiments and feelings, such as we have. We see here hustling to welcome Elizabeth; we see her praising God for his goodness. She was chosen for a very special purpose, however not to be put on a pedestal. We honor her for her spiritual values and for her special role in God's saving plan.

Chapter Three

The Coming Celebrated
(Luke 2:7-20 KJV)

Now WE GO TO the one anniversary that has made our nation's spiritual heritage possible - the anniversary of the birth of Jesus Christ. True, we praise his birth to the world consistently, but it is the ideal opportunity for Christians to insist that had not the good news of Christ come our way, we would not have much, or anything, to celebrate.

The birthday of Jesus Christ is the milestone of all history, not simply of our country's. It is the most significant event that has ever happened, in light of the fact that it marks a time when God himself became man and spoke to us in the person of his Son.

God's mighty acts were known in the past; God's creative power is found in nature; God's provision of our material needs is proof (evidence) of his reality. However none of these contrasts and the fantastic truth of the incarnation, the birth of Jesus Christ.

As a result, God probably contemplated that to convince his creatures once and for all of his love and care, he had to become one of us. When Christ was born into the world the end result was that we should see the Father. "Believe me that I am in the Father and the Father in me," Jesus said (John 14:11).

God isn't a generic, impersonal, unknown force in nature. He is personal; he cares; he wants us to think about it; he wants our love, fellowship, obedience, and worship. That is what Christ's birthday is about. God wants us to take a look at Jesus and to be assured that God is real, that he is like Jesus of Nazareth.

Every Christmas allows us to ponder once again the miracle that happened in the stable of Bethlehem, the amazing miracle that God should come to earth in human flesh. Such an act defies reason but it demands a response.

If anyone refuses to bow before the Creator become man, he relinquishes his life until the end of time (forever). The child of Bethlehem will one day judge us for our response to the realities of the Christmas miracle.

The Circumstances of Jesus Christ's Birth (Luke 2:7 KJV)

Mark tells nothing of the birth of Jesus. Matthew speaks about it only in passing; the presence of the wise men from the east was his central intrigue. John discusses the incarnation of the eternal Word, but records nothing of his birth to the world. Luke, be that as it may, who "followed all things closely" (accurately), is along these lines our key manual for the Christian story.

We may firmly depend on him as having scrupulously drawn from eyewitnesses (1:2, 3) who were as yet available when he wrote. He gives us a most intriguing story.

The birth of Jesus Christ is planned truly by a declaration distributed by the Roman emperor, Caesar Augustus, that people ought to be enrolled for assessment (registered for tax) purposes. Augustus reigned from 31 B.C. to A.D. 14. Jesus was born before King Herod died, 4 B.C.

The execution of the supreme declaration in Syria (of which Judea formed a part) carried Joseph and Mary to Bethlehem, ages before prophesied as the place of Messiah's birth to the world (Micah 5:2). Clearly some time prior Joseph had left his genealogical (ancestral) home and moved to Nazareth in Galilee. Maybe a woodworker (carpenter) may discover greater work there.

Bethlehem was designated "the city of David" and Joseph "was of the house and lineage of David." Jesse, the father of David, lived in Bethlehem (I Sam. 16:1) and this Bethlehem became David's city. It never came to any extraordinary significance.

The list of the urban communities of Judah in Nehemiah 11:25ff. makes no mention of it. Be that as it may, mention of it is made in Ezra 2:21 and Nehemiah 7:26. It remained small; in John 7:42 it is known as a village.

The Lord Jesus didn't get any eminence from the place of his birth to the world. His self-emptying is mirrored even in this. The person who was the bread of life was born in a dark village whose name signifies "the place of bread."

Luke presents the Davidic descent of Christ. The tribes of Israel were divided into families and the families into houses. Joseph had a place not only with the equivalent tribal (ancestral) branch from which David was descended, however explicitly to the house that had David as its founder.

This carries us eye to eye, face to face with the miracle of Christmas. With beautiful simplicity Luke expounds on this wonder of wonders, God manifest in the flesh. Jesus was born into the world in a stable adjoining a inn that was too full to even think about accommodating the fatigued travelers. However likely if Joseph had enough cash, a corner could have been found some place in the inn proper for Mary.

Here is the most emotional evidence of the poverty encompassing the Savior's birth. The family of David is deprived of the position of royalty (deprived the throne) and the crown, they have sunk into destitution, hopelessness, and misery. Usually, extraordinary generosity and delicacy are shown to a woman going to become a mother, but Mary was disregarded and detested. "Every one of the visitors," said Luther, "were serenely dealt with (taken care of) in the inn, however this poor family must go back to the stable the cattle are wont to be."

However the primary concern isn't where Jesus was born. A second-century custom gives a cave as the area of his birth to the world. The mother of the Emperor Constantine in her visit to Palestine searched out the cave and had a splendid church built over it. The straightforward certainty is that Mary found a humble retreat for her infant. The Savior of the world was put in a manger, not a proper place for those who value pomp and prestige.

The world keeps on offering place to those with influence and cash, and thus the truth of Christ's presence is as yet swarmed out, even at Christmas. The embarrassing conditions of our Lord's birth are a striking token of the road we should take if we are to receive him as the Savior from our sins and Lord of our lives. Holding on to selfish desires effectively keeps Christ out, as much as the doors of the inn were closed to Mary and Joseph.

(What dazzles you most about the conditions of Christ's birth? From what you found out about Mary earlier, how would you think she felt when she got dismissed at the inn? For what reason do you think God chose such a subtle, harsh spot for the birth of his Son? What difference do you think it makes that Christ was born in poverty instead of in riches?)

The Proclamation Of The Angel To The Shepherds (Luke 2:8-14 KJV)

There were no TV, web, or radio declarations about the birth of Jesus Christ, however there were a few men who received some answers concerning it in any case. God sent his ambassadors to report what had occurred.

The angel educated the shepherds concerning this child, called "Christ the Lord." The declaration was joined by the expressions of an eminent chorale. In regardless of its obvious effortlessness, this declaration has symbolized the hopes of God's people as far back as it was first given.

The Angel's Appearance (vv. 8, 9)

The child's birth was proclaimed to an ominous gathering of shepherds, not to the amazing leaders of religion and legislative issues. Shepherds for the most part were disdained socially, they were nobodies contrasted with king Herod and his court and the central ministers (priests) and recorders (scribes).

Yet for all their lowliness they clearly were without guile; they were uncomplicated people. God's choice of them to get the good news is fitting with the conditions of Christ's birth in the stable. Maybe among all the people involved with the Bethlehem scene that night they were the most open to receive this new divine revelation.

The shepherds were approaching their work, not suspecting that an angel would appear to them. Whatever the glory of the Lord may have been, it was sufficient to hit them with dread. This was an unexpected, emotional event, enough to incapacitate even the hardest, or the toughest of men.

By and large, flocks were kept outside from April to November, however it was likewise conceivable to do this in winter. Everything relied upon the temperature. We can't demonstrate that Jesus was conceived on December 25, however at any rate it is conceivable that he was. Mary was confined to a stable, which some observe as confirmation that the sheep had cleared it. The birth in the stable blocks the idea of extreme cold.

The Angel is recognized uniquely as "angel of the Lord," not a specific heavenly attendant as Gabriel. Angels appear at the incredible points of the historical backdrop of disclosure.

They show up here, however by God. They showed up after the temptation of Jesus and were with him in Gethsemane. The Risen One was attested by angels and the Lord from heaven was accompanied by angels to the right hand of the Father.

The Angel's Message
(vv. 10-12)

Out of the splendor of the brilliance of the divine glory came a voice. The angel addressed the men, first to calm their feelings of trepidation and second to declare the joyful occasion of Christ's birth. Overwhelmed by God's glory, the shepherds' most prominent need was for calmness of heart and mind.

They couldn't wisely receive the announcement while held with fear. Fear is the outcome of becoming aware of one's shamefulness, unworthiness and sin within the sight of God's holiness. The shepherds needed to be consoled that they were not going judged;, but reassured by the divine angelic messenger, and not struck dead.

As opposed to fear conceivable judgment, the shepherds were to be prepared to receive "good news." That news concerned "a great joy" that was to come to the people. In one sense, the birth of any baby is a glad occasion, but this was something unprecedented, irregular celebration, unusual jubilation was called for by the angel.

In spite of the fact that Jesus was born in a dark stable, people had to know about it. A concealed treasure is a useless treasure. If God had not made this birth be announced by the angels, and had not revealed this treasure to the people, nobody could have desired, much less enjoyed it.

Christians today are the bearers of "good news of a great joy" since they can impart the truth of Christ to other people. The vast majority think about Christ - thousands will sing about him this Christmas - however they are not by and by familiar with the Good news and they have not received the Good news for salvation.

There is no better news in all the world than what the holy messenger (angel) declared: God had sent a Savior into the world. The world was lost, grabbing in haziness. Philosophical insight was useless. The political and military power of Rome couldn't fulfill human longings for fulfillment.

The laws of state and religion were not able change the sadness of people. Something new must be done, or there was no plausibility of improvement.

The Savior's name was "Christ the Lord," that is, God's blessed one of whom the Old Testament prophets had spoken to such an extent. He was brought into the world a child that very day in Bethlehem, however he truly was the Lord of Glory, descended from the Father in heaven.

The reason for his coming is obviously uncovered in "Saviour." He didn't come principally to illuminate mentally or to change the social and political structures. he came to save people from the bondage of personal guilt and condemnation.

The cornerstone of all obvious Christmas festivity is found in the holy messenger's message. It is a message that should be preached each year, obviously, but also consistently. "Good News of a great joy" is exactly what we need to support our flagging spirits; it is the thing that we have to release the burden of sin and despair.

The Praise Of The Heavenly Host
(vv. 13, 14)

As the morning stars sang together when God established the foundation of the earth, and every one of the children of God shouted for joy (Job 38:7), so now at the birth of God's Son the heavenly hosts don't remain before the throne, but they come in numbers down to the earth.

The angels hovered in a mass of light to testify to the shepherds and to the world that God had finally acted to spare humankind. The news was sublime (glorious) to the point that his angelic chorus had to accompany it. This song of praise articulates (utters) the amen of the angel's sermon. "Gloria in Excelsis" was the first century hymn, used as a morning hymn in the Greek church as early as the second or third century.

In the first beginning is always God, and he absolutely provides the gala (feast) of the holy night. Subsequently, the melody of praise rises first from earth to God. The holy angels sing to God "in the highest," that is, above paradise where they dwell. This is a place to which even the angels themselves do not aspire.

The song of praise similarly encompasses the earth. All created intelligences are called upon to praise God. To God be the glory because this child is the gift of his kindness (mercy) and love. That should ever be our subject of praise.

This God over whom the angels exult is "our peace" (Eph. 2:4 NIV). Peace in Hebrew means every good great. The earth will have peace when men being reconciled to God through Christ will have peace in their hearts. In Christ peace is made among God and man between Christian brethren.

The birthday of Christ is the day of peace for those wherever on whom God's favor rests. God's peace isn't given to people because they merit it, but to the undeserving whom he has freely and graciously favored. No wonder the angels broke out in rapturous song; so should we when we receive God's favor in Christ.

(Have you really received God's blessing (gift)? How have you offered your thanks for it? What people do you know who need to believe the good news God has for them in Christ? How might you share it with them? For what reason is even the good news of a Savior difficult to accept? How might you offer glory to God for his magnificent, wonderful gift?)

The Visit Of The Shepherds To The Baby (Luke 2:15-20 NASB)

These verses bring to a peak the narrative of Christ's birth. The story is a complexity between a drab stable and the revelation of God's glory. Presently the scene changes by and by to the stable.

1. They found the child in Bethlehem (vv. 15, 16). how might these men react to the angelic message and song? Would they flee in unbelieving trepidation (fright)? What might you have done? They chose to pursue the angel's word, because they acknowledged his message as from the Lord.

They didn't contend; they assumed that what the angel had told them had truly occurred. They were set up to follow up on God's revelation. So they went rapidly and discovered Jesus with Mary and Joseph.

2. They clarified the message of the Angel (vv. 17, 18). Having seen the child precisely where the angel said they would, they told how they had been coordinated there by the angel. Their

explanation no doubt incorporated the angel's name for the most significant proof of all, for people had long foreseen the coming of Messiah. This is the reason the those who listened in to the shepherds "wondered at what" they said. Clearly their words sounded unrealistic. Might it be able to really be that a child brought into the world here, under these conditions and into a peasant family, was going to be the world's Savior? That was a test of faith.

3. Mary considered the importance of their message (v. 19). Others wondered and Mary pondered. Does this mean they disbelieved and she believed? Maybe so. Luke clearly intends to demonstrate a special response on Mary's part.

She, too, had been told by the angel who her child was to become (Luke 1:32, 33). Now this was additional proof, but might she be able to accept it from these shepherds? There was in reality much for this young mother to consider.

4. They returned full of praise (v. 20). Having been visited by angels, and having found the proof indicated, the shepherds rejoiced. They glorified and praised God because they witnessed with their very own eyes what God had revealed to them. They had seen the newborn child Messiah,

and clearly they believed he was "Christ the Lord." Such faith produces unconstrained praise. This is God's purpose for us all at Christmas.

End: The best Christmas is one in which Christ is honored, loved, and worshiped by obedient, faithful hearts. We needn't bother with tinsel and gifts to do that. The outer trappings of Christmas should not cloud the spiritual realities.

Chapter Four

The Promise Fulfilled
(Luke 2:25-38 KJV)

THE WORLD WAS NOT searching for God to intercede in history in an special way when the Lord Jesus Christ was born, but there were many who foreseen his coming and searched for it eagerly. The innkeeper who turned Joseph and Mary away no clue that God was coming to earth as an infant born to a humble Jewish peasant girl, but some way or another knew when he saw the child this was in fact God's Son.

The complexity between the spiritually dull and the spiritually conscious (aware) proceeds to our very own time. A few people rule out God as a significant factor in their lives. They may even deny his existence, if not that, they imagine that his existence isn't a reality they need to account for in their lives.

Some would concur that there is a God, however they don't anticipate that he should be actively involved with what they are doing. They pooch-pooch the idea that God answers prayer, that God is someone you can talk to, someone you can trust in, someone you can commit your cares and fears to. God is not a living reality to them.

Then again, others put God at the center of their lives. They see him in both the ordinary and in the phenomenal undertakings of life. They converse with him about their nourishment, the nightfall, the rain, and the crops. They give thanks him for sending Jesus Christ to be their Lord and Savior.

They approach him for wisdom to know his will so they can obey. They ask him for faith to trust him when difficult situations arise. In a word, God is the one circumstance in their lives. All else revolves around him.

People settle on decisions that determine if they are spiritually dull or spiritually aware. They choose what they think will be best for them. The spiritually dull think they will be happier going their own way without God; the spiritually aware think the best thing in the world is knowing God, obeying him, and seeing him at work in their lives.

This lesson is about two older elderly people who were spiritually alert (very aware) basically on the grounds that they trusted some old promises God had given. Their faith gave substance to their lives. Without a faith like theirs, life is good for nothing, it is meaningless and empty, like "striving after wind" (Eccl. 2:11).

Simeon, The Devout Man
(Luke 2:25, 26 KJV)

The parents of Jesus fulfilled every one of the prerequisites of the Old Testament laws. They had him circumcised "at the end of eight days" after his birth, at which time they gave him his name, Jesus, in obedience to the command of the angel Gabriel. Jesus is the English change of the Greek form of the Hebrew name Joshua, "whose salvation is Jehovah."

The firstborn of each family was, as according to the law, "redeemed" of the priest of the sanctuary at the price of five shekels. This Mary and Joseph did when they presented their infant to the Lord at the temple in Jerusalem.

Simultaneously - forty-one days after the birth of a child, as per rabbinic law-the prerequisites of "purification" were met by the offering of two turtledoves or pigeons. Ordinarily, the proper offering on such occasions was a yearling lamb for a burnt-offering and a young pigeon or turtledove for a sin - offering, but the people who couldn't bear the cost of such an exorbitant offering were permitted to bring a more affordable one.

For these two purposes the family went from Bethlehem to Jerusalem. The ceremony at the redemption of a firstborn child was straightforward. It consisted of the proper presentation of the child to the priest and two short benedictions - one for the law of redemption and one for the gift of a firstborn son - after which the redemption money was paid.

The rite of purification comprised basically of the sin - offering for the Levitical defilement emblematically attached to the beginning of life, and the burnt-offering that marked the restoration of communion with God. Now all strain was removed, and, as the law put it, they may again partake of sacred offerings.

It was on this occasion that the holy family encountered faithful Simeon and Anna. Unknown to them, God had planned - due to their obedience to the law - to give a one of a kind response (a unique answer) to the longings of these two people. God's timetable was by and by immaculate. He led Simeon and Anna to the temple at the exact time his Son was presented there, so that they could know that God was indeed faithful to his promises.

Simeon's Expectant Faith
(v. 25)

Luke presents Simeon essentially as "a man in Jerusalem." Tradition has looked to interface him with a few celebrated men of a similar name, however there is no hard proof to demonstrate that he was anything over a typical native of the city.

Be that as it may, he bore several recognized stamps as a godly man. He is designated "righteous," which alludes to his relation and bearing to God and man, "devout," which stands contrary to the egotistic vainglory of the Pharisees; and "searching for the consolation of Israel," that is, a longing hope for the fulfillment of great promises of God to Israel.

Furthermore, "the Holy Spirit was upon him," and we will note below the purpose for the Spirit's work in his life. Accordingly, profoundly, Simeon was substantially more than a conventional man.

We don't have the foggiest idea what number of others in Israel shared his genuine character and his hopeful faith, however without a doubt Simeon is singled out in Scripture to be illustrative of numerous others.

The image of the strict and political leaders of the day is disheartening; the people who ought to have been anticipating Messiah were unconcerned and distracted with their own eminence and power in the public eye. The chieftains of Israel were not enthusiastically envisioning Christ's coming, but among the everyday citizens of the day there were people who really dreaded God and believed his promises.

People of hopeful faith (expectant faith) typically stand against the overall sentiments and estimations of the day. They are searching for significance in life as far as God's promises, not as far as earthly yearnings. Today God's people by and by are called upon to look eagerly and hopefully for Christ's coming.

While they anticipate him, they are to be marked by their righteousness, their commitment, their devotion and their yieldedness to the Holy Spirit. Simeon is an example for every one of us.

Simeon's Revelation
(v. 26)

The Holy Spirit revealed to Simeon that he would not pass on before he had seen the Messiah ("the Lord's Christ"). Jesus was an uncommonly normal name among the Jews, since it was the name of their great leader Joshua who had led them to the promised land.

The Hebrew "Messiah" and the Greek "Christ" were names that spoken to the office of Jesus as the blessed prophet, priest, and king.

We are not told the age of Simeon when he got this disclosure, however the ramifications of verse 29 is that he was well along in years. Clearly, his faith had sustained him many years, and God, in a manner of speaking, respected his faith by giving him this special knowledge at the suitable time.

Clearly the revelation agreed with the birth of Jesus. One ancient record says that while reading the Scriptures, Simeon staggered at the verse,

"Behold, a virgin will conceive and bear a son" (Isa. 7:14), and simultaneously got the hint that he ought not die until he had seen it fulfilled.

God's people frequently have been coordinated and educated in a unusual way by the Holy Spirit. The Holy Spirit speaks through both the Word of God, the conditions of life, and the guidance (counsel) of friends. He frequently prompts us as we pray and meditate; he directs us through pastors and teachers.

Simeon had been searching for the Messiah with sincere desire and expectation; presently the Spirit answers that expectation by disclosing to him that he would surely see the promised one with his own eyes; spiritual vision would give way to physical reality.

"Faith is the assurance of things hoped for, the conviction of things not seen" (Heb. 11:1 RSV). Simeon had that kind of faith and God gave him the boundless privilege of seeing his Son, the object of Simeon's faith.

Simeon's Blessing
(Luke 2:27-32 KJV)

These verses burst with the excitement of Simeon's faith fulfilled. This is dynamic, exciting confidence (faith), more fulfilling than anything the world brings to the table. In the event that it took faith for Simeon to hold up "for the consolation of Israel," envision what it took for him to accept that this newborn child would for sure one day be "a light...to Gentiles, and ...glory to...Israel."

Simeon Was Led By The Spirit
(v. 27)

The Holy Spirit was upon Simeon to guide him to the temple at precisely the opportune time. God's affection for this man gave the needed data he expected to see the realization of his expectations. This is the kind of God we can trust to lead us explicitly when we submit our lives to him.

Envision the excitement and expectation with which Simeon moved toward the temple. He was so anxious to find that special child. He could confide in the Holy Spirit to indicate the right one, if there were numerous babies being brought to the temple that day.

There is no lack of faith now, no dithering. His mission supernaturally designated (divinely appointed), and he was led unerringly to the child Jesus when Mary and Joseph brought him into the temple.

Simeon Saw Jesus As God's Salvation For All People
(vv. 28-32)

Simeon really held the child while he burst forward in rapt thanksgiving to God. His previous thought was about his very own life; it was a fitting time to think about the end since the majority of his expectations and been fulfilled; there was nothing more to live for.

Simeon uncovers that his whole purpose for being alive had focused on the expectation of Christ's coming. That purpose had been accomplished.

As a matter of fact, his life of eager (expectant) faith had been one of servanthood to God. He feels under grave, hallowed commitment to the Lord, as one of God's faithful watchmen for the Messiah. Now he talks about being discharged from that obligation.

There is no more requirement for such special servants, since Christ has come. So Simeon thinks about his passing as the end of and dismissal from his servitude to God. The church today needs those unwavering warriors and watchmen who will declare their faith in the truth of Christ's second coming.

Simeon looked at the infant and declared, "mine eyes have seen thy salvation." He knew very well what God's purpose was in the sending of his Son. Now he was really taking a look at the one whose coming he had for such a long time foreseen.

At the point when Simeon saw him, he proclaimed the all inclusiveness (universality) of God's saving plan. He knew that this infant was bound to be more than a great religious teacher. Here was one sent for the salvation of the world.

Simeon's applause, be that as it may, has bot been all around acknowledged; truth be told, few in his time believed him. Not exclusively did the strict leaders neglect to perceive what Simeon saw, they actually murdered the one whom God had sent. In any case, when Jesus returns again it will be unique. World leaders, the rich and the persuasive will stow away in caverns and in the mountains to escape "the wrath of the Lamb" (Rev. 6:15, 16 KJV).

Today despite everything it is conceivable to have the same certain faith that Simeon had about Christ. There still is time for Jesus to be salvation for any person who will trust in him. He is God's salvation for all who confess their sins and receive him into their hearts and lives. Simeon needed to see Messiah with an exceptional desire. God honors that same desire today. He offers Christ to all. Any person who looks for him will find him.

The offer of salvation in Christ is for "all peoples," Simeon announced, for Jews and Gentiles the same. Relatively few Jews would have received the noteworthiness of the Old Testament predictions in connection to the Gentiles.

The Jews thought of Messiah as their very own private belonging, the person who might build up David's great kingdom for them. Be that as it may, Simeon's prophetic understanding goes a long ways past the thin patriotism of the Jews. He valued the full scope of God's salvation plan.

The newborn child Jesus in this noteworthy testimony is called "salvation," "light," and "glory." This is in reality what he brings to those who commit themselves to him.

He saves from sin, moves us from spiritual darkness to light, and lifts us from Satan's kingdom of servitude to sin and gives us "the light of the knowledge of the glory of God even with Christ" (II Cor. 4:6 KJV).

(Articulate your psychological picture of Simeon. How was he? What was there about him that you might want to imitate in your life? What questions do you think may have ambushed him as he hung tight for "the consolation of Israel"? What necessities must you meet before you can be taught and directed by the Holy Spirit?)

(What is your very own personal hope in regard to Jesus Christ? Would you truly like to see him more than all else? Meanwhile, what do you need him to accomplish for you now? Do you have faith to accept that he will do what you ask? What would you be able to praise him for being to you now?)

Simeon's Prophecy
(Luke 2:33-35 KJV)

The glad scene in the temple was not without its strength, since Simeon also prophesied Messiah's future as far as his rejection. Maybe it appears to be strange to interpose this idea here, but the truth of Messiah's suffering was as much a part of the Old Testament disclosure. At the beginning of our Lord's Life, God the Father gave this expansive (broad) picture of what his coming would mean in human experience.

Joseph And Mary Were Surprised
(v. 33)

Simeon's unforeseen appearance and his increasingly surprising deed and words filled the hearts of Joseph and Mary with wonderment. Now they can't completely get a handle on what Simeon has quite recently prophesized, particularly the part about the child being a light to the Gentiles.

Simeon Saw Jesus As Judge And Divider Of Men
(vv. 34, 35)

Simeon's warning includes both the fatal opposition that the divine child was bound to experience both the fatal resistance the national hazards that would unsettle the years to come.

It seems as though the entire history of Christ upon earth were going in quick view before Simeon. However even with that desperate prophecy, Simeon articulated a blessing on Joseph and Mary.

Be that as it may, his prediction was tended to explicitly to Mary. She would endure (and evidently not Joseph) to see the crucifixion of her child.

The image here is of Jesus as both a stone of stumbling ("fall") and a cornerstone for building ("uprising"). The people who fall due to him do so in light of unbelief; the people who rise do as such through faith. Then again, the fall and rising may happen in one person. "He that humbleth himself will be exalteded," said Jesus. Confession of sin and repentance lead to new life.

Jesus will likewise be "a sign that is spoken against." The witness of his words and his deeds was constantly invalidated and rebuked by his own peers. In any case, it was through that resistance to him (opposition to him) that the "thoughts of many hearts" were revealed.

Unbelief came out beyond any confining influence in light of the witness of Christ. He became the point of belief and unbelief. He remains the focal issue for personal decision today. There is no center ground, no middle ground; if an individual doesn't make an open promise to Christ, he is against him.

Our assignment as Christians today is to share Jesus Christ's own witness to himself, with the goal that the hearts of people might be revealed; i.e., regardless of whether they want to accept him or not.

What expectations and fears Mary may have had right now we don't have the foggiest idea, however authentic Simeon revealed to her that the sword of profound personal distress (sorrow) one day would pierce her heart. Mary's battle with this reality during the most recent three years of Jesus Christ's life more likely than not been agonizing.

Anna, The Aged Prophetess
(Luke 2:36-38 KJV)

The presentation of Jesus to the Lord was additionally set apart by the recognition and witness of a matured (aged) widow, a prophetess named Anna. Here again we perceive how God declared the noteworthiness of what had occurred at Bethlehem through the lips of one who had been faithful to him for a lifetime. Anna is a distinctive picture of what the "golden years" can be for God's people.

Anna's Spiritual Discipline
(vv. 36, 37)

We have no pedigree for Simeon, but we do for Anna. In her home the ancestral family history had been saved. Since she was from a tribe (Asher) that had not come back to Palestine, it is deduced that she had some family qualification. In any case, there are different realities about her authentic (godly) way of life.

She was a widow whose early barrenness had been trailed by a long life of lone grieving. Notwithstanding, her spiritual vitality and walk with God were strong to such an extent that she gave herself totally to fasting and prayer. Her aloneness was honored by the presence of God. She moreover gained comfort from the promise of Messiah's coming.

Anna's Rejoicing And Her Witness
(v. 38)

To Simeon's song of praise is added Anna's on this extraordinary day. This prophetess right then and there perceived the child Jesus as the fulfillment of the expectations (hopes) of those who were searching for the redemption of Jerusalem. No big surprise she gave thanks to God. For a considerable length of time, almost certainly, some portion of her petitions had been for Messiah's coming.

Now her supplications were answered. being subsequently convinced, she imparted (shared with others) to others the good news of what God had done. Clearly, numerous others had been praying as she had. They needed to know that God's anointed Son had come.

(Of what intention was Simeon's prediction? How is the situation of Anna an encouragement to faith in the times of seeming darkness? How might you share your faith in the coming to Christ again?)

End: God's people maintained faith through long hundreds of years of persecution. Since they did, they were able to perceive God's intervention on their benefit when it came. Today we need similar characteristics of long-suffering and patience, even as we anticipate the Lord's return.

Chapter Five

Jesus Affirms His Sonship
(Luke 2:39-52 KJV)

THE GREATER PART OF history of the life of Jesus is committed to the most recent three years of his life, the long periods of his public ministry, his torturous killing (crucifixion), and his resurrection. Actually, around one-fourth of the space in the four-gospels portrays the most recent seven day stretch of his life.

Thusly, in the complete picture we have just fourteen verses in the gospel of Luke that reveal to us anything about Jesus as a youngster and youth. This doesn't imply that his adolescence was insignificant, however it means that Jesus Christ's suffering and death for our sins are intended to be our central concern.

Indeed, even in this concise look at those early years the record is certain that Jesus was not an ordinary child. We have noticed the miraculous reality of his virgin birth. Here we consider him to be a twelve-year old astonishing his elders with his knowledge (wisdom). Simultaneously clearly his parents obviously were not ready (not prepared) for his unusual gifts.

Aside from the supernatural, be that as it may, there is human 'component of his godly childhood and upbringing. God's Son was naturally in to and brought up in an ordinary human family setting. He didn't show up full-developed on the scene, prepared to articulate God's truth. Jesus experienced a similar adolescence and youth that are typical of most children.

This demonstrates God's high regard for the family as an institution. In a day when many grown-ups grumble that their relationships (marriages) aren't working, and when youngsters whine about the restrictions of the parents, this image of our Lord's family life is refreshing.

There is no proof that God's fundamental plan for parents and youngsters has changed since the times of Christ's youth. Wise, loving parents and obedient children continue being what God desires. Truly, Jesus was an exceptionally wise child, but his essential spiritual and emotional needs were met by his parents.

The Bible doesn't disclose to us what strains they needed to survive. We experience many unique social pressures upon family life today. Our commitment to build our families on God's foundation is necessary if we are to furnish our children with the kind of healthy environment that Jesus grew up in.

The Childhood Of Jesus
(Luke 2:39, 40 KJV)

Historically and traditionally, there has been a ton of interest about the childhood of Jesus. Numerous whimsical stories have been told about assumed miracles that he executed as a youngster. There are totally unusual (out of character) with the scriptural records.

In these two verses we have all that the Bible has to say about his childhood. This is adequate data; we need do whatever it takes not to decorate it. Nothing is added to Christ's stature by contributing stories for which there is no scriptural warrant.

Jesus Grew Up In Nazareth
(v. 39)

Luke's record passes promptly from the introduction of the child Jesus in the temple to his childhood in Nazareth. In any case, in Matthew 2 we have two noteworthy occasions recorded that happened preceding the settling of the family in Nazareth: the visit of the wise men to Bethlehem and the trip of the family to Egypt to avoid king Herod's deadly vengeance (his murderous revenge). They remained there until Herod died (4 B.C.).

Joseph clearly wanted to return to Bethlehem in Judea (Matt. 2:22 KJV), however he was cautioned in a dream not to do that, so he went rather to Nazareth. He had valid justification to fear Archelaus, the child of Herod, since he had ordered the slaughter (massacre) of 3,000 of his countrymen.

For Luke's purposes, the stay in Egypt probably must have been too short to even think about influencing in any capacity the human development of our Lord. So he essentially discloses to us that Nazareth was the place Jesus grew up.

Nazareth was eighty miles (four days' journey) north of Jerusalem in the territory of Galilee, ruled by another son of Herod, Antipas. For reasons unknown, the town was regarded with hatred (cf. John 1:46). However it delighted in a flawless area enclosed by slopes. Toward the south lies the Plain of Esdraelon and the road to Jerusalem.

Toward the east is the Valley of the Jordan; toward the north, the mountains rise in a steady progression to the summit of Hermon; toward the west, the ridge of Carmel and the Mediterranean Sea. It was the focal point of a mixed population.

From the standpoint of location, it was a perfect place to grow up. For Joseph, Nazareth represented to selusion and safety. Later on, be that as it may, not long after Jesus started his public ministry, the people of the place where he grew up (his hometown) rejected him and attempted to kill him (Luke 4:16-30).

Jesus Was Strong Physically, Intellectually, And Spiritually (v. 40)

This verse abridges the advancement of Jesus between the ages of two and twelve. In one sense Jesus developed equivalent to any typical child would. He didn't land on earth totally endowed with unending wisdom. The key proclamation here basically is that Jesus grew. This implies he progressed in development beginning with one stage then onto the next.

The suggestion is that Jesus enjoyed a healthy childhood; he enjoyed a strong body, a sound personality (sound mind), and the blessing of the Lord. These, obviously, were the Lord's endowments to him. The emphasis of the Bible isn't on his physical characteristics; the majority of that is left to the creative mind of the painters.

Nonetheless, it would not be right to expect that he endured through the usual harsh times of childhood, and furthermore the standard sicknesses.

What dazzles or impresses the scriptural author is his wisdom and his grace before the Lord. This developing youngster was remarkable in his spiritual and mental capacities. Luke gives one delineation of this in the verses to follow. Once more even with this story the Bible doesn't depict the boy Jesus as intelligent or spoiled.

We know, in any case, that in one significant trademark he was not the same as other children; only he of all children at any point born enjoyed an immaculate, spotless, sinless, stainless childhood.

So the biblical record is straightforward and to the point; as opposed to report some stunning

Dr. John Thomas Wylie

miracle, it tells of growth, growth not in popularity (fame) however in spiritual stature; growth not in wealth, because his parents were poor; growth not in being obliged as somebody unique, because he was regarded as the child of a humble carpenter.

Jesus' Visit To The Temple (Luke 2:41-50 KJV)

Luke gives us here the only account of the one single event known about Christ between his birth and his baptism. This episode demonstrates the common concern of his parents, the scholarly stature of this child of twelve, and most significant, his sense of divine mission and obedience to that mission at such an early age.

Jesus Stayed Behind To Talk With The Teachers (vv. 41-47)

Mary and Joseph were accustomed with to attend the Feast of the Passover at Jerusalem consistently. This was the great celebration of the Hebrew year. It went on for seven days. It was one of the three yearly feasts that each Israelite, if he could, attended in Jerusalem.

It not only remembered a national deliverance - the "passing over" of Israel by the destroying angel when the Jews were hostages in Egypt - but was accepted to verify a similar mercy for all Jews thereafter.

The Passover itself was eaten uniquely by males, but the seven day stretch of the feast was a period of widespread rejoicing, so spouses were inclined to take their wives, as well as their children, with them.

So when Jesus was twelve, the age at which the obligations of the law became binding upon him, he came for the first time. He was currently viewed as a child of the law, having contemplated the Scriptures from the age of five. At twelve the Jewish child was presented by his father in the synagogue.

The twelfth year was viewed as a significant boundary year. From that point on boys were obligated to learn a trade for their own support. Up to this age they were designated "little"; from now on, "grown up."

Mary and Joseph stayed in Jerusalem the full seven days and after that began for home. They had gone a day's voyage when they found that Jesus was not in the company among their kinsfolk and colleagues, as they had assumed.

They were going with numerous others coming back to Nazareth and close by towns, the young men and youngsters most likely walking together in gatherings, and the more seasoned people, a considerable lot of them on mules, independent from anyone else.

In this manner it was not irregular for guardians and youngsters to be isolated.

They remembered their steps and on the third day in the wake of arriving at the city they found Jesus in the temple, sitting amidst the teachers, both hearing them and asking them inquiries. All were astounded at his comprehension and answers.

This simple story of a lost boy stimulates a note of compassion for us, in light of the fact that numerous parents have experienced a comparable encounter. Now and again, children meander away carelessly; in others, they intentionally keep running off. On account of the boy Jesus, there is no proof of unpleasantness (meanness).

Luke doesn't fault either the boy or his parents for what occurred. Maybe Jesus ought to have asked his parents' permission. He could have informed them, but in God's plan it was appropriate that the intelligence (wisdom) of Jesus should be highlighted by his disappearance.

You can well envision the thrill and exuberance of Jesus on his first visit to Jerusalem and the temple. This was no ordinary occasion; it was the most emotional thing that had happened as far as he can tell to this point. He most likely pursued the inspiration of the moment, existing apart from everything else, the senses of his heart, the driving forces of his inclination, and the novel virtuoso (genius) that was a part of him.

The primary focal point of Luke's record is on what Jesus was doing in the temple. There were rooms off the temple courts where the teachers, the famous doctors of the law, met their understudies (pupils), explained the law, and responded to questions. A huge piece of the rabbinical books comprises of answers given by rabbis to their understudies' inquiries.

Jesus was there to ask and learn, not to cross-examine the doctors. He was not an inquisitive tourist taking in the sights, sounds, and scents of the huge city. Or maybe, he needed to hear the truth of God explained. He was there in all humility and reverence to his elders, as an energetic hearted, gifted student.

His eagerness encouraged the reverence of the teachers and his bearing won their regard and their love. They gave him a seat so they may have a further, closer talk with him.

He tuned in and posed inquiries. At the point when the profundity of his wisdom wound up evident, the teachers posed Jesus a few inquiries. The rabbis set much store by the comments of young children. As indicated by one of their Proverbs, God's Word is to be received from the mouth of childhood like God's Word from the mouth of Moses and the Sanhedrin.

Along these lines, the twelve teachers were amazed by this youth. The word deciphered "amazed" signifies "to be next to oneself," the most elevated level of amazement or joy. This due to his comprehension all in all and particularly his answers. Jesus maybe gave the doctors a lesson in teaching and explaining God's laws.

How would we represent his unusual insight?: First, as a child Jesus was happy to set aside effort to contemplate, to remember, to ponder God's word. His parents assumed a role in this, as well, since they were his first teachers. They were faithful in encouraging and in enforcing his study.

Second, he was starting to show his divine nature. Jesus was not just a brilliant youth; he consolidated the aftereffects of human examination with the natural bits of knowledge that were a part of his deity. He amazed the teachers not as some sort of human hotshot, but because in his situation his divine endowments were being revealed.

Jesus Defended What He Had Done
(vv. 48-50)

The rabbis and teachers in the temple obviously didn't reprimand Jesus for being there alone without his folks. Be that as it may, Joseph and Mary were bewildered when they discovered Jesus among the teachers. Following three days' searching to find him, quiet and glad, in so august a presence.

Mary speaks the expressions of delicate rebuke from a mother's heart. She feels hurt due to the tension they have suffered in view of his non-attendance (absence). They had known his obedience to this point.

Maybe their every day commonality with him had by one way or another blunted any feeling that their child would have been diverse as a result of his heavenly beginning. Here was their first sign that the child Jesus was unique.

Mary posed an inquiry, uncovering their throbbing heart. Jesus didn't offer an immediate response, but himself posed two inquiries to legitimize (justify) what he had done. Not their losing of him but rather their looking for him offers Jesus the opportunity to raise the basic issue behind his conduct. Jesus was not aware of any disregard or disobedience. The inferred reprimand of his folks was undeserved for his situation.

These are the principal recorded expressions of the Lord Jesus Christ. They show unmistakably his sense of divine Sonship.

His answer isn't at all ill bred; it sounds accurate with the age of the young, yet in its simplicity it incorporates the majority of the mysterious depths of the incarnation of God in human substance.

Simply, Jesus pronounces he has a higher need (a higher priority); he should be in his Father's house. The Greek content peruses actually, "that I should be in the of my Father." There is no noun for the definite article "the." The importance may either be "in the house of" or "in the affairs of" my Father. Since the first question of Jesus communicates shock (surprise) that Mary didn't have the foggiest idea where to discover him, it appears to be likely that the reference is to his Father's home, or the temple.

The clarification of the boy consolidates perfect dignity with perfect humility. It fits the totality of Jesus' life and ministry. "Did you not know" implies that Mary and Joseph should have recalled his divine origin and mission, "I must" sets out the principle of self-sacrifice that led him at last to the cross.

By this statement he accepts the Father's claim on his life as being higher than that of Joseph and Mary. He had acted out of internal need, out of most noteworthy obligation, his duty. He was consistently doing not his very own will, however the will of the Father.

Now Mary and Joseph couldn't assemble the pieces (they did not get it). The angel had revealed to them both that the virgin-born child was to be God's Messiah. In any case, by one way or another in the course of recent years (twelve years) this message had maybe become diminish, in light of the fact that Jesus had behaved like other young men, without taint of sin. He had at no other time caused them nervousness or horror. However they couldn't comprehend the meaning of his questions.

The Youth Of Jesus
(Luke 2:51, 52 NIV)

These verses incorporate the following eighteen years of our Lord's life. Albeit so little is said about them, we can't ignore them without a thought.

He Obeyed His Parents
(v. 51)

This is the huge reality about Jesus as a youthful grown-up. It has to do with his relationship to his earthly parents. In the wisdom of God this is the thing that he has chosen to tell us.

We additionally realize that Jesus learned the carpenter's trade (Mark 6:3) and clearly this is the thing that he accomplished for eighteen of his twenty-one grown-up years.

This was a part of his willful accommodation (his voluntary submission). This statement demonstrates that what happened when he was twelve was not insubordination nor disobedience. Jesus was the ideal or perfect example of childhood, youth, and young adulthood.

While Jesus carried on with this peaceful, uneventful life, procuring cash to purchase bread and meat and garments, his mother though much about her son and what he had said. The experience in the temple taught her to be progressively industrious (more diligent). The word "kept" demonstrates cautious preservation. She pressed to her heart what she heard from Jesus.

He Grew In The Sight Of God And Man (v. 52)

Jesus showed early maturity, but he continued to increase in knowledge and wisdom. This was pleasing to both God and men. Jesus developed in the fullest harmony between his body ("stature") and his mind.

It was development to full holiness of life. He commanded the approval of men because he had not yet reproved them by his word. As Jesus developed into more fuller comprehension of his divine mission and relationship, so did the Father's pleasure in him.

(What impresses you most about Jesus during his adolescence and youth? About his parents? What model is there here for you to follow? Are there examples for your life to pursue here? What are the duties of parents found here, and those of youngsters?)

To portray thirty years of Messiah's life in such a concise degree barely appears to be fitting, but this says something regarding his humility, his willingness "to be made like his brethren in each regard, with the goal that he may turn become a merciful and faithful high priest" (Heb. 2:17 RSV). He surrendered the exposure of his deity with the goal that he may experience all that we do. Completely aware of his Sonship with the Father, the Lord Jesus blessed family life and everyday work with his very own example.

Chapter Six

Jesus Accepts His Calling
(Mark 1:4-13 RSV)

HIGH AND LOW SNAPSHOTS (moments) of life often come close together. The experience of a good time is no assurance against misery or depression quickly following. Indeed, even in the spiritual domain we might be on the mountain top at one minute and in the valley of gloom the following.

A few people vainly trust in a consistent enthusiastic high plane of living. Those who enjoy liquor, tranquilizes (drugs) for instance, say they do so on the grounds that it gives them a passing "high." Some books and strategies for therapy claim to have the option to enable people to live over the low moments that other people experience.

Life can turn into a distraught quest for break from the cruel substances of life. Indeed, even diversion and amusement can be types of break from the real world. Sexual ventures are a part of this drive to search for something that will be over the daily practice (routine) and the dull. TV watching can ship us to a universe of make-believe.

Be that as it may, regardless of what we attempt, there is the inescapable frustration, the enthusiastic void cup. This is a part of our human experience, and it is absurd to attempt to escape it. Rather than looking for a break, we have to sustain our hearts and minds to address the difficulties, the tests, the harsh occasions of life.

Christians are not shielded from these tests, however they are not compelled to meet them all alone on their own strength. This lesson portrays how the Lord Jesus Christ went from the high purpose of his Father's approval at his immersion to the depressed place of being tempted by Satan in the wilderness.

This is a real temptation; Jesus suffered it to demonstrate his full identity with us. He recognized what it meant to confront serious tests. He didn't live on a emotional high, but rather took the worst the enemy (the devil) could toss at him.

In this manner, as he lives in Christians he can meet their issues too. At the point when a

Christian feels low, when he is hit by something intense, (something tough) he can claim the power and presence of Jesus Christ. Jesus experienced everything, with the goal that we might not have to experience anything alone.

The Ministry Of John The Baptizer (Mark 1:4-8 NASB)

Mark's gospel starts with the record of how John the baptizer preached repentance preceding the public ministry of Jesus. Mark incorporates nothing about the birth of Jesus in his telling the Savior's life, which is the briefest of the four accounts.

Mark's gospel has been known as the good news of action or the gospel of action on account of the manner in which he tells his story. It is assumed that he got his information from Peter.

These verses inform in a brief scope regarding what John preached, how the people responded to his preaching, how John lived, and how he prepared the way for Jesus Christ. You will recall from our study of the birth of Christ in Luke that John's birth was fortunately revealed to Zechariah.

The angel said that John would "turn many of the sons of Israel to the Lord." Zechariah prophesied that his son would "go before the Lord to prepare his ways, to give knowledge of salvation to his people in the forgiveness of their sins" (Luke 1:76, 77 NASB).

What John Preached
(v. 4)

John is distinguished as "the baptizer" (not the baptist) due to the great number of people he baptized. He showed up "in the wilderness," that is, where he grew up (Luke 1:80), which was not strictly a desert, but the fruitless (barren) Judean slopes overlooking the Dead Sea.

We don't know at what age he ventured out from home to live there all by himself, but he was most likely thirty when he started to preach. His preaching was not restricted to one spot, for Luke lets us know "he went into all the region about the Jordan" (3:3).

John preached "a baptism of repentance for the forgiveness of sins." Baptism itself was not something new for the Jews. Washing in the Jordan River had been a sacred image in any event since the times of Naaman the leper (II Kings 5). In any case, John's Baptism was very extraordinary; it was something new on the religious scene. His preaching required repentance of one's sins.

Repentance implies fundamentally to alter one's perspective; to change one's mind, it means a turning. The picture is of an individual going one way, turning, and after that switching course.

Spiritually, this alludes to one's demeanor (attitude) toward sin. The person who repents recognizes the truth about his sin, an offense against God's holiness that brings the simply sentence of judgment.

The change of mind is a change away from self-righteousness and independence of God and toward accepting God's will and his standards of holiness. The repentant individual is more than sorry he has trespassed (sinned); he is determined to forsake his sin. The change of mind leads to a change of heart, which leads to a change of conduct.

Repentance is the first move towards getting forgiveness for our sins. If an individual doesn't repent, he can't be forgiven by God. Since sin is against God, only he can forgive it. Be that as it may, God doesn't forgive based on human opinion; he is not like Santa Claus.

God is governed by holiness and justice, as well as by love. He forgives because he is loving, but his just and righteousness necessitate that the heathen (sinner) must repent.

Forgiveness means God starts from scratch (He wipes the slate clean); he doesn't hold our sins against us. An individual can't know God in this life and can't foresee paradise unless he is forgiven. The unrepentant, the unforgiven are bound to spend eternity isolated, separated from God. Sin brings God's only judgment upon us. Hence, if our sins are not forgiven, we will perish eternally.

The people of John's day were very much aware of the consequences of sin. The whole Old Testament sacrificial framework was a clear reminder of what must be done to atone for their sins. However the penances themselves were of no profit (no avail), unless the worshiper's heart was truly repentant.

The Old Testament prophets reliably preached repentance on account of the many personal and social sins in the land. John was following in this example. The religious system of Israel must be made personal by these spokesmen for the Lord.

The Response To John's Preaching
(v. 5)

John's preaching pulled in a wide group of spectators from the wide audience of Judea and the city of Jerusalem. People from varying backgrounds ran to hear him. He was unsparing in his condemnation of them. The religious leaders themselves didn't get away from his allegations (accusations).

Whoever they were, and whatever their needs, John baptized them in the river when they confessed their sins. This was a striking scene for the Jews who were so strongly proud of their religious legacy. So far as we probably am aware, none of the prophets baptized publicly.

There was tradition of a public call for repentance and confession. The people who responded were under genuine spiritual conviction. It requires great fearlessness or courage to step out before a crowd of in crowd of people who know you, and confess you sins.

This is particularly true if you have been making an outward religious profession. Religious people are the hardest to convert.

Here was genuine change. Here was open and humble sorrow for sin. Here were people making sacred vows to change their way of living. Here were people claiming God's forgiveness. Here were people and willing ready to make a public declaration of their change by walking into the waters of the Jordan. This was unheard of in Israel.

Why such a dramatic work of God at this time? This was a preparation for the Messiah. John was preaching the way for Jesus. God's Son had come to launch his public ministry. He would teach clearly God's principles of holiness.

John was preaching get the people spiritually prepared for the coming of one who was perfectly holy. Repentance and confession were the only right way to get ready for the Son of God.

John's Life Style
(v. 6)

John's way of life fit in with the demands he was making of people (cf. Luke 3:10-14). He was not a comfortable evangelist living as indicated by the standards of the world. His attire and his nourishment were unmistakably basic; there was nothing rich about him.

He spurned the fine garments of the rich Pharisees; rather, he wore unpleasant fabric and calfskin (rough cloth and leather). John lived off the land. His eating regimen comprised of honey and locusts. He refused to indulge his physical appetite. One's spiritual sensitivity is heightened by self-denial. There is nothing amiss with standard nourishment and garments, however now and again treating the flesh all the more rigorously makes us increasingly open to the voice of the Lord.

John cultivated a meager way of life to be completely open to God and to authenticate his message. The people could see that he backed up his words with his life. There was nothing deceptive (hypocritical) about him.

John's Witness To Jesus Christ
(vv. 7, 8)

John's preaching pointed to Christ because he demanded repentance and confession, however he additionally gave public witness explicitly to the coming Messiah. John roared against sin, but when discussing Jesus he was exceedingly humble.

Humility is the hallmark of his statement here. It is difficult for a well known evangelist, encompassed by swarms of people, to state that a much more noteworthy preacher is coming. In any case, John enthusiastically did that. He dismissed his very own claim for fame for the sake of Christ (cf. John 3:30).

The coming Messiah was so great in contrast with John that the baptizer felt he wasn't even adequate to loosen Messiah's sandals. This statement surely stunned the recently repentant people. It stirred their interest. Who could be so much mightier than the baptizer himself? John's lowliness (his humility) was in itself a pointer, a sign to Christ.

To make the differentiation among himself and Christ considerably more noteworthy, John essentially said his repentance wasn't as critical as that which Messiah would bring. John didn't downsize his baptism, but he said Christ's would be of an different kind by and large, so extraordinary that it resembled contrasting water and fire (cf. Matt. 3:11; Luke 3:16). Fire, obviously, is an image of the Holy Spirit.

This examination further reveals the need of John's preaching and witness. The Holy

Spirit came and lived in people. This was a dumbfounding idea. It required new spiritual molding. Jesus Christ would usher in a new element of spirituality. The Holy Spirit came on the believers at Pentecost like tongues of fire (Acts 2:3). To be prepared for this, the people needed to heed John's call for repentance and confession.

(Had you been in swarm of people, what might you have felt about John? Do you think his way of life would have made you awkward? Why? Shouldn't something be said about his preaching? Would his statement about the man to come have excited your interest? In what sense would you be able to be one who "prepares the way for the Lord"? What kind of preparation do people need today to prepare to receive Jesus Christ?)

The Baptism And Temptation Of Jesus (Mark 1:9-13 KJV)

Just as Mark condensed the ministry of John, contrasted with the treatment by Matthew, Luke, and John, so he likewise gives the most limited account of the baptism and temptation of Jesus. For instance, he doesn't give Satan's three temptations in detail. Be that as it may, you can't miss this fundamental effect of these events, despite the fact that Mark omits a portion of the facts found elsewhere.

John Baptized Jesus
(v. 9)

While the spiritual revival was going on under John's ministry, the Lord Jesus went from his home at Nazareth to the scene where John was baptizing. The others came to be baptized as an indication of the spiritual change that had been created in their hearts. They confessed their sins and declared their intention to change.

Jesus, presently around thirty years old, didn't need to be baptized for that reason. He had no sins to confess; he didn't have to or need to repent. John perceived this about him and did not want to baptize Jesus (cf. Matt. 3:14). Why at that point was Jesus baptized? His answer: "To fulfill all righteousness" (Matt. 3:15). After bearing that clarification, John baptized him.

Jesus came in obedience to his Father's will. For him to "fulfill all righteousness" signifies doing what the Father commanded. His submersion (baptism) likewise demonstrated his eagerness to be related to the people who were in effect spiritually prepared to receive him.

He went to the Jordan like all the rest, despite the fact that he was deep down and apparently perfect. Be that as it may, there he stood with the crowds of sinners listening to John's preaching. He was for sure "numbered with the transgressors" (Isa. 53:12) now, despite the fact that he was not one of them:

John, obviously, was an evangelist of righteous nature. By coming to him, Jesus supported John's call for repentance and his call for godly living. John was on the right track to state that he should have been baptized by Jesus, strictly speaking, but for this situation Jesus willingly submitted to that outward indication of true spiritual vitality.

The Spirit And The Father Signified His Deity (vv. 10, 11)

Now we get familiar with why Jesus was baptized. In spite of the fact that he went to the river as one of the group, his baptism was joined by outward signs that didn't pursue the baptism of any other person. Jesus was baptized not only to be related to sinners, but additionally to get a public witness to his divinity (his deity).

That witness took two forms. In the first place, the Holy Spirit came upon him like a dove; second, the voice of the Father originated from paradise. The words of the Father affirmed his special relation to Jesus and his pleasure with his Son.

We can't be certain beyond a shadow of a doubt about this, but clearly these signs were planned and intended essentially for Jesus himself and secondarily for John. We don't have a clue whether others were available, but if they were, regardless of whether or not they saw the dove and heard the voice.

These signs are the initiation of God the Son into his ministry. They resemble getting the crown of the confirmation, endorsement, and blessing of the Father and the Spirit for his coming ministry, suffering, and death.

For us today, these signs are total confirmation (absolute proof) of Christ's divinity. He was not only a decent man filled with a thought based on his very own preference that he would change Israel. As a young person of twelve, he knew about his Father's special mission. Without a doubt, for a long time (eighteen years) he contemplated, studied, and prayed.

Now at his baptism Jesus received unmistakable witness to the internal promptings of the Holy Spirit. As completely human, he required this help and support. He knew what was ahead, however having been "born in the likeness of men: (Phil. 2:7), he needed the specific help of the Spirit and the Father for his unique mission.

"Thou art my beloved Son" stands as full proof that Jesus was surely God's Messiah, not one among many children of God, but the only begotten of the Father. He was God in bodily form (God Incarnate). In Jesus of Nazareth was the full embodiment of divinity. This is the foundation or cornerstone of Christian doctrine.

Satan Tempted Jesus
(vv. 12, 13)

Immediately after the dove landed on Jesus, and the voice of the Father reverberated from paradise, Jesus was dove into awful temptation. The purpose of Satan's allurement was correctly reality that had been affirmed at his baptism: his deity.

Satan needed to disappoint and frustrate Christ's crucial mission from the start, and he looked to do that by causing questions in the mind of Jesus about his unique and special relation to the Father.

Three explicit temptations are recorded in Luke and Matthew. In two of them, Satan blatantly charged, "If you are the Son of God..." Satan wanted Jesus to reject obedience to the Father; he needed him to reject his Father's special care, even during forty days of temptation.

Be that as it may, for each situation, if Jesus had pursued Satan's recommendation (suggestions) and performed a miracle, it would have implied a denial of God and a selling out to Satan.

In the final test, Satan offered Jesus the kingdoms of the world as a byproduct of his loyalty (in return for his allegiance). This would have meant no salvation for us.

For each situation, Jesus turned aside Satan's intrigue with a word from Scripture. He knew God's will perfectly in light of the fact that he knew his word. He was not vulnerable against the enemy. Sacred writing (Scripture) was in his heart, and the angels encouraged him in the fight.

Along these lines, in spite of the fact that Jesus experienced the most exceedingly terrible, he was victorious. He experienced the valley of temptation to demonstrate his obedience to God and to demonstrate to us that he knows what our temptations are like. In this manner, we can call upon him for help (cf. Heb. 4:15, 16).

(How does the believer's baptism today please the Father? When does the Holy Spirit come upon a Christian? (Cf. Lady. 3:2-5, 14; 4:5; John 7:37-39). What plan does God make for you when you are tempted? For what reason does temptation so regularly pursue a spiritual high point?)

Conclusion: Jesus began his public ministry with a act of humility, with the seal of divine endorsement (divine approval), and with the testing of the fallen angel (the enemy, the devil). All through his three years of serving God, his obedience to the Father was tried, but he continued to sustain his faith by humble dependence on the Holy Spirit. He prayed and he walked in every day fellowship with God. Today we can tap the same sources of spiritual power to live a victorious Christian life.

Chapter Seven

Jesus Declares His Mission
(Luke 4:14-24 NIV)

———————

To HAVE A MISSION in life means having a fundamental reason (a basic purpose) that explains every decision you have to make. (It would be interesting now to request that friends state what their mission in life is).

Having a mission means that you concentrate on it; you will not accomplish things that would degrade your fulfillment of it. To land at your mission life requires unswerving steadfastness and exceptional order.

Tragically, many people have no clue what their mission in life is. For some, there is no particular point to living, nothing to be accomplished, no goal to reach. They are for the most part putting in time, or in any event, killing it. They are out to remain alive; their main goal is to get by, to take care of their tabs, to remain healthy, to have some good times, to retire easily.

Obviously, other people do have more significant standards throughout everyday life. They need to contribute something to the advancement and betterment of society. They want to help people. Many choose to go into medicine, education, and politics for that reason. Researchers are persuaded to discover new developments and new fixes. That is their mission in life.

The vast majority of us attempt to find purpose and meaning in what we do, however except if a person recognizes the truth of God, he will miss the essential purpose and motivation behind his being here. Such a large number of goals in life are conceited, or they are man-centered. We come up short on a feeling of a higher calling, a feeling of responsibility to the Creator who put us here.

The Savior of men had a remarkable mission to achieve. Every person who knows Christ can have that same ability to know east from west. It becomes out of basic commitment to God's will. God can give us an assortment of missions, in the event that we are sensitive to his leading. What could be better than to go for and achieve the goal of pleasing God above everything else, regardless of what our own money related and profession objectives are?

In this lesson we will perceive how Jesus explained his mission to those who observed him. We also can have a positive witness for God, if we are able to articulate our feelings about our obedience to God's will.

The Ministry Of Jesus
(Luke 4:14, 15 NIV)

In these two verses Luke summarizes the ministry of the Lord Jesus Christ. They serve to present the particular story of his ministry at Nazareth. From the realities here we gain proficiency with the fundamental character of Christ's mission.

After the baptism and temptation in the wilderness, Jesus stayed some time in Jerusalem and Judea. Luke excludes totally this prior ministry and devotes the following six chapters of his gospel to Christ's ministry in Galilee.

Both Matthew and Mark give the incident at Nazareth, which we study in this lesson, as happening a much later in the Galilean ministry. Luke records Jesus' reference to his work in Capernaum (v. 23) and in this way was very much aware that he was recording the event at Nazareth out of its chronological order.

Apparently he put it right early in his gospel since it is a key passage that demonstrates the deeds and expressions (words) of Christ's mission that will be stressed in his gospel.

Jesus' Reputation Grew
(v. 14)

Jesus was anointed by the Spirit at his baptism, led by the Spirit into the wilderness where he was tempted, and enabled by the Spirit to carry on his ministry. "The power of the Spirit" was the hallmark of his life. He was not left on a self-initiated ministry; he didn't leave from the assets of strength provided gave by his heavenly Father.

He sent the same Holy Spirit to his followers (disciples) at Pentecost. He gives the same Holy Spirit to the people who have faith in him today. The Spirit's power is accessible for anyone to attain his spiritual mission in life. Without the indwelling Spirit, it is extremely unlikely a believer can be faithful to God's calling.

Jesus was not ignored; people recognized his unique gifts. They spread the news quickly. The "report" was not carried on TV or in the papers or web; it was spread by listening in on others' conversations (word of mouth). Any place travelers and traders assembled, they discussed what Jesus of Nazareth was saying and doing.

The housewives in the market places without a doubt were filled with inquiries concerning this new prophet in Galilee. It was a time of public expectancy, and the news spread immediately even without the broad communications (mass media) of today.

Jesus Taught The People
(v. 15)

Jesus was an teacher in the customary Jewish sense. He didn't have a school and he didn't have an earned specialist's degree, but he taught in the synagogues. His teaching concerned God's principles in Scripture. His teaching was intended to bring about spiritual change; it was not principally scholastic; it was not cold strict religious theory.

Being an teacher is a high calling, one with great obligation, responsibility, and accountability. It is a commendable mission in life. From the expressions of Christ in the Bible we know how he exemplified good teaching. Here, in summary, we note that his teaching was valued (appreciated) by the people.

Presumably his naturalness, his simplicity, his adoration, and his straightforwardness intrigued the people. People were familiar with gathering around the teachers, in light of the fact that there was no system of public education.

This was their only method for learning. The Lord Jesus offered new light about issues of essential concern. Thank God his teaching has been preserved for us, so that we may study it and be drawn nearer (closer) to God by it. As we learn of him, we will be moved as the people of his day were.

Jesus' Teaching At Nazareth
(Luke 4:16-24 KJV)

We center now around one teaching occurrence, in which Jesus unmistakably revealed what his mission in life was. These verses show how he instructed (taught) from the Old Testament and how he interpreted the prophecies with regard to himself.

We will likewise take note of how his teaching produced hostility as well as acclaim. What Jesus taught about himself and his mission has never been all around acknowledged (universally accepted), on the grounds that his teaching requires moral and spiritual change.

More than certainties of religion are included. Jesus Christ's mission was to preach and teach so people would come into a saving relationship with God by faith.

Jesus Read In The Synagogue
(v. 16)

Jesus lived least twenty-eight years in Nazareth, so he was well known there. This was the place where he grew up (his hometown). Going to the synagogue there was his life long habit. In spite of the fact that he was the Son of God, Jesus faithfully kept up the observance of regular worship with his family and fellow townspeople.

The end of the synagogue always faced Jerusalem. On one side of the room sat the men; on the other, behind a cross section (the lattice), sat the hidden veiled women. The central article of furniture was the chest, or ark, of painted wood, before which generally hung a curtain.

This ark contained the sacred rolls of the law and the prophets. Before the ark and facing the people were the chief seats for the ruler of the synagogue, the elders, and the person who led the devotions. In the middle of the synagogue was the bema, or platform, on which there was a desk and from which the law was read.

There were no consistently appointed readers nor preachers. It was the custom of the ruler to welcome any distinguished or competent individual for the service. The exposition of the Scriptures was not left to risk, in any case, on the grounds that there existed wherever a class of prepared understudies (trained students), the scribes and rabbis.

The rabbis gave their services free (at any rate that was the ideal) and they earned their living by practicing some common (secular) trade. The scribes were in any case copyists of the Scriptures, who made the duplicates for the synagogues and furthermore for people who could afford to buy them. They were likewise legal counselors, for the law of Moses was the rule that everyone must follow. In any case, their main duty was to expound the Scriptures in the synagogues. They were as prominent in the synagogues as the priests were in the sanctuary (temple).

The Prophecy Of Isaiah
(vv. 17-19)

The sabbath day service started at 9 o'clock. The reader presented the Eighteen Prayers and the people replied with their Amen. Next came the first lesson of the day, the people rising and reciting the words after the reader. Another lesson pursued. The books had been partitioned by the copyists (Scribes) into well-organized lessons, and these were read in regular order. The reader consistently stood, and next to him was the translator (interpreter).

The holy compositions (Sacred writings) were in Hebrew and this was converted into Aramaic, the normal language of the nation. At that point came the exhortation, delivered sitting.

On this specific event the lesson was from Isaiah 61:1, 2, a particular prescience about the coming of Messiah. These verses depict Messiah's mission in general terms of spiritual restoration (renewal). It speaks about people being poor, mistreated, blind, oppressed, and in bondage.

This is the common lot of mankind. The human condition for the most part is certainly not a wonderful one. The desolates of sin are horrible to see. A great many people suffer the results of covetousness, mercilessness, brutality, mistreatment, oppression and sickness.

This prophecy demonstrates unmistakably that God intended to take care of the suffering of mankind. The most exceedingly terrible of the human condition is an invitation for God to intervene. God doesn't forsake his own (his people). He clarified when he redeemed his people from bondage in Egypt.

He clarified when he sent his Son as a man to take care of our basic needs. God's love and care sparkle splendidly in this prophecy.

The conditions are terrible and grim, taking a look at then physically and spiritually. You can't separate the two in these verses. People are destitution stricken and dazzle and in bondage spiritually as well as physically. God offers hope as a way out of the most worst terrible oppression of all, the oppression of sin.

The verses were a sparkling encouraging beacon to the Jews of Christ's time; they remain so today. In any case, they are not to be taken in any case politically - as some have attempted to do - in light of the fact that Jesus clarified that this kingdom was not of this world.

He was not an advocator of savagery and upheaval (revolution and violence). Jesus brought the answer to smashing oppression of the human spirit by offering God's forgiving. At the point when he comes back again to build up his earthly kingdom, we will see true freedom for the hostages (captives) and the oppressed.

Jesus Christ's mission portrayed several different ways here: to preach good news, to proclaim release, to set at liberty, to proclaim the acceptable year of the Lord. This passage is a part of the general topic of Isaiah 49-66, the person, office, sufferings, and triumph of Messiah.

We find in our Lord's life that he related to the necessities of the humble, the oppressed, the outcasts of society. Some he healed. A portion of the visually impaired were made to see. he didn't heal all and he didn't void the detainment facilities, but by his preaching and teaching he offered a new way, a new lifestyle, and the everyday citizens readily and gladly responded.

This is a freedom and a healing that are a higher priority than political freedom and physical healing. The freedom and healing of the human soul from the imprisonment (captivity) and abuse (oppression) of spiritual servitude and spiritual blindness is Christ's highest mission. Anyone today can come to him to have those needs met. This is what Jesus Christ proclaims.

Jesus Himself Fulfilled It
(vv. 20, 21)

The people were eagerly and excitedly looking for "the acceptable year of the Lord," that is, the year graciously chosen by God as the time of his favor to men. They knew what the prophets had said. This golden age was going to be wonderful. Envision then their response when they heard Jesus say that that day had shown up (arrived); the Scriptures he had quite recently perused had been fulfilled.

Jesus plainly demonstrated that "he" was the one upon whom the Spirit of the Lord rested; "he" was the one anointed by the Lord; "he" was the one sent by God to proclaim freedom. This is further proof of the deity of Jesus Christ. He took the prophecies of Messiah and applied them to himself. There can be no mixing up or mistaking the role he took upon himself.

Before his own loved ones, directly in his own locale, Jesus made the most stunning case they had ever heard, This was no customary lesson. They had heard the words previously, but they had never heard any of the scribes or rabbis state, "These prophecies are now fulfilled in me."

Luke writes that Jesus "began to say to them," in this manner demonstrating that Jesus proceeded to give a more full clarification than we have here. Be that as it may, the central matter is the fulfillment of the prophecy in the person of Jesus Christ.

The hopes and aspirations of the people could now be acknowledged in the one standing before them. You can envision how hypnotized, how spellbound they more likely than not when they heard the place where they heard their hometown boy claim to be the Messiah of the Lord. There could be no conceivable misconception of what his mission in life was to be.

Jesus' Claim Mystified The People
(v. 22)

Now there was only awe and thankfulness all through the assemblage. But then there was likewise disarray. What truly dazzled the people? They acknowledged both what he had to say and how he said it; his words were "gracious," that is, they ministered hope and solace to the individuals who received them.

All things considered, the old promises continued burning in the hearts of the people, but Jesus didn't work up false expectations (false hopes), he didn't purposely lead the people to anticipate that a mass movement to political freedom. He offered new spiritual hope.

Be that as it may, the people started to think about how the carpenter's child could say such words. They couldn't account for such grace and wisdom coming from their very own backyard, in a manner of speaking. They had built up a different impression of Messiah.

They couldn't accept the fact that for about three decades he had lived, eaten, and worshiped with them. Now he professes to be the Messiah! How could this be?

So they debated the issue that proceeds to our own time: Who is Jesus Christ and what did he come to do? Numerous researchers say, as a result, he was simply another carpenter who had distinctly built up a sense of religious mission, which the people rejected.

Jesus to them is essentially Joseph's son. Then again, as we have noticed, the Bible says Joseph's son was without a doubt God's promised Messiah, the one sent from God to be the Savior of the world. Joseph's son on the human level couldn't begin to fulfill the prophecies that describe Messiah's mission.

This is the reason why the people stumbled. They were not prepared to accept the fact that God could come to earth as a woodworker's (carpenter's) son and accomplished his saving purposes.

Jesus' Anticipated Their Rejection Of Him (vv. 23, 24)

At the start of his mission Jesus knew what was coming. He knew the adulation of the home people would not last; it would before long go to brutal disdain. So he began to test the spiritual issues that prompted his rejection.

The issue was straightforward: If this man was truly the Messiah, he would perform some prominent signs like he had done in Capernaum. They had found out about those miracles. Now they could hope to see a portion of the equivalent. Joseph's son, in the event that he was somebody uncommon, would perform for them. They needed to see a miracle-worker.

The people where Jesus grew up evidently got no bit of leeway from that in light of the fact that their hearts were not readied. Jesus was not satisfactory to them. They couldn't overcome any issues between the human and the divine in Jesus.

They saw only his humankind, not his deity. The urgent issue was spiritual visual impairment (spiritual blindness), not freedom from oppression by the Romans. Jesus demonstrated that by telling around two Old Testament cases in which a prophet abandoned his own nation to offer a blessing to an outsider whose faith conquered prejudice (vv. 24-27).

The visual deficiency of the Nazarenes appeared in their jealousy of the people of Capernaum and their desire of the distinction of Jesus, who was one of their own. At the point when Jesus revealed their actual emotions, they attempted to slaughter (kill) him by tossing him over a cliff (v. 29). They couldn't acknowledge presentation of their actual, but true spiritual condition.

They were prisoners surely, not to Rome, however to their very own pride and sin. Jesus Christ came to proclaim freedom and they rejected the messenger. In this manner, they couldn't know true freedom. He plainly expressed his mission, they would not accept what he came to do.

(What conceivable example for your own life would you be able to discover in the mission of Jesus? Is the Christian's mission preaching? Why or Why not? How might you locate a scriptural harmony between the social and spiritual demands of the gospel? In the event that you had to characterize/define what Jesus wants to do on the planet today, what might you say? How would you represent the Nazareth's rejection of Jesus? Do you see any counterparts of this mentality today?)

Chapter Eight

Jesus Calls His Disciples
(Luke 5:1-11 KJV)

THE BIBLE IS FILLED up with stories about people who received a unique call from God. Abraham, Moses, Isaiah, Jeremiah, Paul, and the apostles. But today many individuals don't think about the significance of their lives as far as obedience to a call from the Lord. The overarching design today is for individuals to settle on their own decisions, as opposed to allow God to do the choosing.

The possibility of a call has been limited to individuals who are looking for a strict employment. Subsequently, for instance, an individual may say, "God didn't call me to be a minister, so I'm allowed to pick some other vocation."

Be that as it may, the person who is genuinely committed to Jesus Christ looks for his will for each choice (or decision). There is no part of life that we can mind our own business. Jesus is Lord of all. He may choose a teacher or peaceful vocation for you, or he may choose a teaching or medicinal profession, but the significant thing for the Christian is to be certain that what he is doing is in light of Jesus Christ's bearing.

There are such a significant number of potential outcomes before people today, such a significant number of voices on the planet clamoring for consideration: "Do this! Purchase this!" The fight for Christian discipleship must be battled in vocation decisions, but additionally in decisions of marriage, spending our cash, utilizing our time, etc. There is a "call" to follow Jesus Christ in these issues too.

Jesus called twelve men to go into a relationship with himself. Today he calls all individuals to clench hand to repentance and faith, at that point of proceeding with teaching. That is the most fulfilling life there is, basically is to be Christ's submissive, committed disciple, regardless of what your activity or profession is.

Jesus can make any work into spiritual help because he can change our dispositions. If we follow him, he will give us the spiritual vitality we need to succeed.

The central issue is, Where are the people who are willing to forsake all to follow Christ? The world has nothing to offer that can contrast and the joy of living in this kind of relationship with Christ. This lesson tells what Jesus did to win his first disciples. He is just as powerful to win us over to himself today.

Jesus Christ's Teaching Of The Crowds (Luke 5:1-3 KJV)

Here is a typical scene that denoted the years of our Lord's popularity. But then, as we will see, even as Jesus taught the crowds he was searching for the individuals who might participate in a closer relation with him.

The People Wanted To Hear God's Word (v. 1)

There was something in particular about the quality of Christ's teaching that went about as a magnet toward the people. They ran from wherever to hear him. They perceived his lessons as "the Word of God." It was authoritative and it was given graciously and lovingly. Jesus was God's Word in bodily form (The Word Incarnate). In him, grace and truth were superbly combined.

The Christian's privilege today is to share the same winsomeness of Christ, a same truth of God's

Word. His teaching is accessible in a manner that has never been known, yet multitudes are ignorant of it.

This is on the grounds that they do not have the personal touch, they lack someone to sit down and study God's word with them. People who won't make a special effort to go to a preaching service frequently are pulled in to home Bible studies, or to an individual study with a Christian.

On this event, the groups jammed around Jesus as he taught on the shores of Gennesaret (Galilee). This was a ground-breaking (powerful) mass movement. Be that as it may, Jesus exercised love and patience with the pressure of the crowd.

The tension built essentially on the grounds that people at the back edges (the rear fringes) of the group of spectators couldn't hear what Jesus was saying. They needed to draw nearer, so they pushed and pushed, while Jesus attempted to hold fast at the edge of the water against this floodtide of humanity.

Maybe Christians today need to pray to God for a revival of hunger after God's truth. If his word isn't the believer's main nourishment, at that point there is a spiritual issue present. No Christian can grow without devouring the Word of God. The soil wherein discipleship is rooted must be the faithful study of the Scripture.

Jesus Taught Them From The Boat
(vv. 2, 3)

Two void angling boats were secured along the lake. The one belonged to Simon Peter and the other likely to his angling accomplices. Be that as it may, these men clearly were giving no consideration to what was happening close by. While the groups squeezed nearer to hear Jesus, the anglers continued cleaning their nets.

But, Jesus got into Peter's pontoon in any case and requested to take him out from shore. He proceeded with his teaching session from that point. What a weird scene it more likely than not been! Unable to persevere through the smothering stifling oppression of the crowd, Jesus didn't abandon them. He fulfilled their aching for the word of life transforming a modest angling pontoon into a lesson.

He now had Peter among his audience members. Rather than washing his nets, Peter was currently compelled to sit in the vessel with Jesus and hear him out: Already there is some sign here about what Jesus had as a top priority. He was tending to hoards, but he was going for one individual.

Strikingly enough, Jesus was not going for someone who had rushed after him in the crowd, however for someone who was doing his day by day schedule: cleaning nets following a late evening's angling.

Simon's pontoon and Simon himself took need now. Jesus took his pontoon so as to call men; later he would utilize their catch of fish to outline how he was going to utilize them to get men. Peter was ignorant of the majority of this, obviously, however as we think back we can perceive how Jesus attracts us to himself through the ordinary issues of life.

Along these lines, we ought to be alert and delicate to his voice consistently, in any event, when we're doing our standard errands. Who knows when Jesus will choose to utilize an individual and his activity for his glory? Peter was looking the other way, in a manner of speaking, but the Lord was looking for him. At the point when Jesus ventured into his pontoon that was the start of the defining moment in his life.

We can accept that Peter was even grim and cantankerous in light of a night's drudge to no end. However, despite the fact that he is nauseated with the lake and his work, he has something to do that appeared to be a little errand. So he responded when Jesus solicited some help from him. These two men were familiar (cf. John 1:42; Luke 4:38, 39). Jesus most likely requested Simon's pontoon on account of this companionship.

At any rate, Peter concurred quickly.

At that point he needed to tune in to the message. What Jesus discussed isn't recorded here, however we would not be right in accepting there was something said for Peter's advantage.

He was washing his nets, giving no consideration to the word preached, but now with Jesus in his vessel he can't escape from the Lord's teaching.

(For what reason do you think people rushed to hear Jesus teach? How could your church's Bible teaching service be made progressively appealing? How might you intrigue more individuals in studying God's Word? What are a few instances of things we give more regard for than the Scriptures? By what method can even fundamental things, similar to Peter's washing his nets, be a hindrance to offering time to Bible study?)

The Huge Catch Of Fish
(Luke 5:4-7 KJV)

The message to the crowd completed, Jesus had something further to do. He abandoned the majority to Simon and his accomplices in the angling industry. He had a command for them to obey and a promise to claim. This was a part of his loving plan to win them away from their vocation to himself.

Jesus Directed The Fishing
(vv. 4, 5)

Jesus Christ's words more likely than not caught Peter off guard, he himself was most likely feeling better at this point. What is unusual, notwithstanding, is that Jesus would dare to know something about angling. It more likely than not appeared to these anglers that he knew next to nothing about their work.

He was a carpenter in terms of professional career and he originated from an inland town. By and by, he instructed Peter to move out into the deeper water and start angling once more.

This was an inappropriate time and an inappropriate place. Great angling requires darkness and the fish are in the shores, not in the deep waters. In any case, the Lord Jesus was keen on getting disciples, not fish. So his bearing of the angling activity is gone for the anglers. Jesus is going to reveal himself as Lord over the anglers as well as the fish.

Jesus gave a command to Peter and Peter had one major issue with the offer. They had quite recently angled the entire night and had not gotten a solitary fish. Now after their disappointment and dissatisfaction, are they to take a stab at an inappropriate time and place. As indicated by both explanation and experience, this was miserable.

This was a serious test for Peter. He would have wanted to remain in the vessel, tuning in to Jesus, but now he is called to obey. With the command Jesus likewise gave the promise of a catch, but did Peter have enough faith in Jesus to accept that they would really find something? The majority of his normal impulses and preparing would reveal to him this was pointless, however Peter chose to comply.

Peter obeyed basically at the expression of the Lord Jesus. This is the sign of teaching. Submission and Obedience is required in any event, when the master's command has neither rhyme nor reason. The disciple's confidence is inspired by the master's promise, not by his own resourcefulness. Peter defeated his own hesitance, his own reasons, and chose to let down the nets.

"Toiled all night and took nothing" was the snag, but faith in Peter's heart conquered it. He required this as a major aspect of his preparation, for he normally relied upon his very own strength and wisdom.

Now he was going to discover that faith in Christ's promise is the only power a believer needs. The probability of accomplishment rests in obedience to what Christ tells us to do. "But at your word" is the only reason we need.

Both Boats Were Filled
(vv. 6, 7)

When Peter obeyed the master, he accomplished an amazing outcome. Most likely he expected to come up with practically nothing, yet very separated from his appearances, the Lord Jesus created a miracle.

There were such a large number of fish got that the nets started to tear. the accomplices in the other pontoon were gathered and they came to help. Together they filled the two vessels with such a significant number of fish that the boats started to sink.

Here was sufficient confirmation of Christ's power as well as of the blessings of discipleship. The disciple acts in obedience to his master.

For this situation, Peter was not confounded by doing what appeared to be a pointless errand; rather, he was blessed a long ways past (far beyond) what he could have anticipated. The Christian who does what Jesus Christ commands will in due time find that his net has been filled, in a manner of speaking.

Jesus had taken something at which these men were experts and showed how he could overrule what may be known as the anglers' theory of probability. There are no restrictions to what he can do.

Some portion of his ministry in building disciples was to persuade these men of his divinity (deity). The followers' (disciple's) trust is just as substantial as the one in whom it is set.

(Request that believer's share a few experiences where God addressed them about accomplishing something that appeared to be incomprehensible. What is the connection between such tests and one's development in faith? What sort of excuses do people as a rule make to the Lord? For what reason does it appear to be more diligently to obey Christ than your very own mind and preparing? What would you be able to do to encourage someone to make a complete commitment to Jesus Christ?)

The Fishermen Become Disciples
(Luke 5:8-11 NIV)

The center transformed from the fish, the bursting nets, and the sinking pontoons to the Savior himself. This supernatural occurrence (miracle) carried the anglers up close and personal with spiritual reality. They needed to react somehow or another. Jesus was after their faithfulness, their allegiance, and this is the thing that he gained.

Peter Confessed His Sinfulness
(v. 8)

Peter fallen at the feet of Jesus and beseeched him to leave. He saw a huge gap between himself and Christ. He realized he had gone up against the celestial superbness (divinity), in control as well as in holiness. His familiarity with Christ's holiness brought his very own sin strikingly before him. This is ever the consequence of genuine spiritual conviction.

Discipleship starts with such a confession of unworthiness. No disciple says he is fit for his calling. No individual can come to Christ and volunteer based on his own integrity.

Contrasted with the inimitable glory of Christ, nobody is fit, yet he calls us to himself. At the point when Peter perceived the truth about Jesus, he didn't from the start request to go along with him. Rather, he requested that Christ leave.

The purpose behind this request was essentially that Peter couldn't make sense of a methods whereby he may make himself deserving of Christ's company. Maybe following quite a while of unbending spiritual discipline he may be commendable (worthy), but Peter knew his own heart at that moment and he knew that his own sin would keep him from Christ.

Notwithstanding, Peter likewise had no thought of divine grace. He was under the law of Old Testament morality. He had not yet learned of the forgiveness that is accessible through Christ the Savior. Now Christ brought him guilt, not forgiveness. Hence, he wanted to get away from Jesus.

The Miracle Astonished Them
(vv. 9, 10a)

The majority of the anglers were shocked by what had occurred. James and John were accomplices with Simon Peter in the business. The record here recounts the association Peter made in his mind between the supernatural occurrence (miracle) and the divinity of Christ. By suggestion, the others were thinking a similar way.

In any case, Peter made the underlying confession becoming out of the occurrence. Regularly, he expressed what others were thinking. Once in a while he became overly enthusiastic, however here he was on strong ground.

Jesus Promised A New Career
(v. 10b)

The Lord Jesus responded to Simon's urgent request (plea) and confession. In the first place, he tended himself to Peter's dread. What was Peter terrified of? Most likely of some imminent coming divine judgment.

This would be resulting to his own conviction of sin. When a person goes under such conviction, he fears the results. The test of a genuine acknowledgment of sin is whether or not a person fears judgment.

If there is no sense of approaching judgment, then there has been no true conviction. The spiritually stirred sinner will go to an acknowledgment that God is just in punishing him for his transgression (sin).

Having witnessed a mighty miracle, Peter could without much of a stretch have anticipated that Jesus should do something frightful. He had not yet received (grasped) a handle on the Savior's love and benevolence (mercy). In this way, Jesus consoled him: "Don't be afraid." When we know Christ does without a doubt receive sinful men, forgives them and doesn't condemn them, we can be liberated (set free) from the dread of judgment.

Second, Jesus gave Peter a look at his very own future. Rather than being an angler, he would be a catcher of men (a fisher of men). Peter's life would take a sensational turn under the Savior's call. His old vocation would be given up for a new spiritual ministry under the leadership of Jesus Christ.

"Catching men" for Peter would mean being involved with ministering to their spiritual needs. He would turn into the rock of the church at Jerusalem. His preaching would flip around the city or turn it upside down. We know nothing of Peter's spiritual dread at this point.

Jesus doesn't disclose to him what he should do to prepare for his new vocation. Now it was sufficient to calm his fears, assure him of acceptance, and promise him a fulfilling ministry.

They Followed Jesus Christ
(v. 11)

Jesus Christ's promise of a new vocation was given to Peter, but when they got to shore each of the three men followed Jesus. Their respond to

Christ's call was emotional: "They left everything." This implied their activity and their business basically. Jesus extended to no employment opportunity, no job security, no salary increases, no benefits plans. He offered only himself. The new disciples teaches simply "followed him."

Discipleship may or may not mean a new vocation. Clearly, Christ is calling many to serve him in a full-time Christian profession. There are numerous requirements and openings today for pastors, ministers, instructors, youth laborers, Christian training laborer, etc. His call to these vocations must be focal in the church and Sunday School.

However, every Christian is under commitment to follow Jesus Christ. Discipleship is a proceeding with relationship of submission and obedience to Jesus Christ. Following means doing what he says. Leaving everything means giving up your will to Jesus Christ as a matter of first importance. When that is done, Jesus Christ guides us to specific places and circles of service.

(For what reason do you think Jesus chose working men to be his first disciples? For what reason is it important for a potential follower to confess his very own sin and unworthiness first?

What number of various ways do you think a follower can "catch men"? Do you think your church is making a sufficient showing of focusing on full-time Christian professions?)

End: The Lord Jesus calls us to the obedience of faith, the experience of his forgiving grace, and a life of walking with him. There can be no teaching without these spiritual elements.

Jesus didn't bring down his standards to attract disciples. He chose men who were fit for self-denial. The Christian faith rests on self-denying love of the Son of God; it is experienced deepest by the individuals who follow that example.

Chapter Nine

Power Over The Demonic (Temperance)
(Mark 1:21-34 KJV)

IN THE PAST FEW years many people have gone from unbelief to conviction with respect to the presence of the demonic. They have recognized the truth of the concealed (unseen) spirit world. Alongside this change has come a resurgence of enthusiasm for spiritism, black magic, Satanism, and dark enchantment (witchcraft).

Many people have turned out to be enchanted with clairvoyant marvels, and even Christians have been taken in on account of the supposed "spiritual" components included.

One reason for this change is that people are searching for something to have faith in; there is a spiritual void in their lives. Realism won't fill this void in their souls. They are scanning for some connection with inconspicuous reality, since they have not discovered anything in the material world to fulfill them.

This has been a peculiar, sudden improvement, in light of the fact that in the period of present day science people as far as anyone knows put the old superstitions behind them. This should be the point at which you put stock in only that which you could see, feel, touch, and experience in physical ways. The research facility strategy underscored truth as that which was measurable and observable. The people who had confidence in the spirit world were laughed out of court.

Now, in any case, modern educated people counsel horoscopes and stargazers (astrologers). They visit mediums and compose witches' covens and Satanic "places of worship (Satanic churches)." Great colleges explore the truth of clairvoyant forces.

The Christian puts stock in the truth of the satanic without being superstitious. The Bible reveals Satan as the leader of the spirit universe of fallen angels and evil spirits. Jesus Christ and the apostles experienced evil spirits (demonics).

They didn't vanish in the first century. The Christian has no compelling reason to counsel horoscopes and palm readers; the Christian possesses the Holy Spirit within him to guide him. The Bible commands believers to stay away from any meddling with divination or with sorcery of any kind.

This lesson shows how Jesus met and defeated the demonic spirits. Hence, no Christian need be in dread of or in bondage to the demonics. Jesus Christ is stronger than Satan; he is stronger than any of the malevolent demonic powers Satan has released in this world.

The Unclean Spirit Cast Out
(Mark 1:21-28 KJV)

Mark records at the start of Christ's ministry an exciting test of the spirit world against Jesus Christ. The test happened in full public visibility in the synagogue at Capernaum. Jesus Christ emerged the victor, and the people began to evaluate the implications of this demonstration of his divine power.

Jesus Taught With Authority
(vv. 21, 22)

Following the formal call of Peter, Andrew, James, and John by the sea of Galilee, Jesus brought them into the city of Capernaum, which was a seaport on the lake. It was the angling town where Jesus lived during his Galilean ministry. It was additionally a customs center, the central command of a royal authority, and the area of a significant synagogue.

On the sabbath Jesus went into the synagogue and taught (see Chapter Seven for details of the synagogue service). We don't have the foggiest idea about the Scripture lesson he utilized on this event, however we are sure that as indicated by the custom he read and explained a book from the Old Testament.

The response of the individuals is significant; they were surprised at the teaching of Jesus. Mark gives the explanation behind their shock: Jesus taught with authority, "and not as the scribes." This is a noteworthy articulation, since it shows that the scribes were content to think about different elucidations of the law. As a result, they were legal advisors (lawyers), and for this situation they couldn't come to definitive yea or nay.

On the other hand, Jesus stated, "This is the way...this is the thing that you ought to accept ...this is the thing that you ought to do." Jesus didn't offer the people an assortment of feelings; he was not an academic scientist, but a proclaimer of truth. He didn't allow the people to pick and choose what was the truth; he disclosed to them what it was.

Lamentably, the strategy for the recorders still exists today. It is thought prejudiced, unacademic, and informal to declare truth. Free-thought (the view that reality can't be known without a doubt) holds influence, even in certain churches.

Strict researchers let us know not to be unyielding. Then, people need some truth they can build their lives on. This is the thing that Jesus Christ offers: authoritative truth. He is the authority because he is the truth.

Consequently, Christians need make no expression of remorse for helping people to find truth in Scripture. God has revealed truth in his promise; it is the Christian's privilege and duty to share it. Along these lines Christians can bring the truth, expectation, and peace of Christ to many who are hungry spiritually.

The Demon Challenged Jesus
(vv. 23, 24)

On some occasions the demon-possessed were excluded from society in light of their rough conduct (cf. Mark. 5:1-13). In any case, here we have a case of a demon-possessed man who evidently was acting normally in the synagogue.

We can't dare to portray a careful example that will fit each case of demon-possession. Today is very dangerous to attempt to characterize specific sorts of conduct to demon-possession

Regardless of the spate of books and films about demon-possession, it isn't something to play with. We should approach the subject and the phenomenon with caution. Much damage (harm) has been done by untimely analysis.

Then again, we should take into account the probability of demon-possession, in purported agnostic societies abroad as well as in edified, refined America. The fallen angel (the devil) has no restrictions with respect to where, when, and how he will work.

For this situation, maybe the man would have gone unnoticed, then again, actually the unclean spirit challenged Jesus. Here was an experience between the holy and the unholy, between the clean and the unclean, between the Son of God and Satan.

Satan previously had tried Jesus in the wilderness; now he assaults him through one of his agents, an unclean spirit dwelling in a human being.

We can't exactly identify evil presences, demons, or unclean spirits, other than to say they are a spirit manifestation of Satan himself. They are sent by Satan and serve him. Why a few people are demon-possessed had we don't have the foggiest idea, in spite of the fact that an individual starts to fiddle with spiritism, dark enchantment, etc, he progressively opens himself to Satanic influence and conceivably to demon-possession.

A few people intentionally request that Satan assume control over their lives. They want to experience the profundities of unholiness and wickedness.

We have to distinguish between demon-possession and being tested by Satan. No Christian can be controlled by a evil spirit (demon), but he can be the subject of Satanic assaults, even as Christ seemed to be.

The devil utilizes different strategies to subvert Christians, extending from the trickiness of "an angel of light" (II Cor. 11:14) to the direct attacks of a "roaring lion" (I Pet. 5:8). For the majority of his deceptions and assaults the Christian needs "the whole armor of God" (Eph. 6:11).

We know nothing about the background of the man Jesus experienced in the synagogue, but clearly something that Jesus taught triggered this respond. The demon recognized the divinity and the power of Jesus Christ.

The demon likewise knew about Christ's mission. The unclean spirit's information originated from Satan, obviously. Satan knew from his fall that God would redeem humanity by sending his Son as Savior of the world.

Satan's main intention was to foil God's saving plan. The demons were very much aware of what was happening in this astronomical battle among God and Satan (cf. James 2:19). There was no uncertainty that Jesus had come to defeat Satan and to destroy his power.

Now the unclean spirit was voicing truth through a human instrument, truth which up 'til now was not known to anybody. Here we are given a look into the scope of the mission of Jesus Christ. His mission would not go untested; this was a life and death struggle. There was more at stake than the condition of the man in the synagogue.

Jesus Commanded The Unclean Spirit To Depart (vv. 25, 26)

Jesus acknowledged the demand straightforwardly and addressed the unclean spirit. His reproach was vital on the grounds that Satan's power was free to move around at will. The man was being utilized as a device, a tool. Jesus along these lines didn't address the man, however to the voice of the evil presence leaving the man.

This reproach was important to show publicly (openly) that Jesus Christ would assume the assault of the satanic. The people in the gathering lived in dread of devils; they had confidence in their existence. this was not something they were new to. consequently, Jesus advised the unclean spirit to go unchecked.

The evil spirit writhed the man and yelled noisily, yet he withdrew and there was harmony. This regularly is the example today. There is wild physical conduct under satanic assaults. Regularly the individual suffers enormously for no clear reason.

For this situation we see one last evil attack (demoic attack), yet the result was clear. Jesus Christ was in charge. He constrained the unclean spirit to leave.

Only the power of Jesus Christ is strong enough and able to deliver. His power must be claimed for this horrible suffering (terrible affliction). Despite the fact that there are many aspects of demon that remains puzzling, the Christian need not be frightful. What is sure is that Christ can assert his power to deliver.

The People Were Amazed
(vv. 27, 28)

The people had never observed such a showing of divine power. They thought the evil spirits (demons) were incomparable, but here was one who might control and compel even the demons. So the entire gathering was buzzing with questions. Might they be able to truly accept what had just happened?

Christ's teaching was basic as was his dealing with the unclean spirit. Once more, the focal note was his authority. When commanded, something occurred. There was no uncertainty, no hesitation in his way.

The shock of the people grew out of Christ's complete control of the circumstance. "Indeed, even the unclean spirits obey him" is a comment that reveals to this point the people considered the demons to be outside anyone's ability to control.

Now Christ had accepted Satan's open demand or challenge and had won. No big surprise his notoriety spread all through Galilee. This was a part of God's plan to attest the deity of his Son. The combat had to happen on this level.

Individuals living in terror must be delivered. They needed to witness the demonstration of God's matchless, supremacy in Christ. The Lord's Messiah was attested by defeating the satanic (demonic).

Would demons be able to be cast out today (exorcism)? There is recharged enthusiasm for this ministry. It has happened; missionaries have had to call on Jesus Christ to deliver the demon-possessed. It is happening with expanding recurrence in the U.S. Be that as it may, once more, this isn't something to be trifled with nor taken lightly.

Incredible insight is required; extraordinary consideration and caution are required. Express gratitude toward God that the power of Christ is accessible today and that his name is still strong enough to force the demons to flee.

(In what aspects of your life do you sense a test to Jesus Christ's authority? How can his word become more authoritative to you? What would you be able to do when you feel an issue is too much for you? For what reason do you think a some Christians are defeated? How can you help them?

The Sick And The Demon-Possessed Are Healed
(Mark 1:29-34 NIV)

Mark tells of another personal healing done by Christ and afterward shows how the city of Capernaum responded to Christ. There is a lot of consolation (encouragement) here to look for the personal touch from Jesus Christ. His love and care shine in these verses.

Jesus Healed Peter's Mother-In-Law
(vv. 29-31)

Obviously, Jesus used Peter's house as his home while he was in Capernaum. They went straightforwardly from the synagogue to the house. There they discovered Peter's relative (mother-in-law) wiped out with a fever.

Most likely in view of what had simply occurred in the synagogue, they enlightened Jesus concerning the woman's sickness. It more likely than not appeared the best thing to do for her. If Jesus could cast out evil spirits (demons), it is intelligent to expect that he could take care of this ailment.

Jesus responded to her faith and healed her. She was alright with the goal that she could continue her responsibilities in the home. So Jesus and his companions had a supper together there. You can well envision what the discussion around the table more likely than not had been about that night.

This episode shows how Jesus fits into the typical life and routine of the city and the family unit of Peter and Andrew. He identified completely with the needs and aspirations of the people.

He didn't seclude himself as a prima donna, but came to help and to care. His divine power was showed in this setting of human need.

The Crowds Came To Jesus
And He Healed Many
(vv. 32-34)

In the wake of casting out the evil presence (demon) and healing Peter's relative (mother-in-law), Jesus was met by hordes of individuals at the doorway of the house. It was currently dusk of the sabbath day. What a day that had been. The city actually was buzzing with excitement.

If you had been one of those tormented by sickness and malevolence spirits (demons), you would have been frantic to find Jesus. We can without much of a stretch account for the large number that accumulated at the doorway.

This is a realistic picture of suffering humankind. A similar suffering goes on today. God has used his people to meet spiritual and physical needs. Be that as it may, the facts demonstrate that many people suffer today with no knowledge of Jesus Christ. They don't have the foggiest idea where to go to find him.

They surrender all expectations (hope) regarding religion without hope and healing. They need answers; the only answer is simply the person of Jesus Christ. Our churches can fill in as Peter's house did, as a gathering place for the people who need to find Jesus Christ.

Jesus didn't turn the people aside; he had no available time; he didn't guide them to return when time was convenient. He could have been unwinding, relaxing with his companions, but he went out and healed the sick and cast out demons.

Simultaneously, he put the top on further evil presence upheavals. There was to be no discussion with them now. The explanation: "since they knew him."

This is a weird explanation. We know from the past episode that the unclean spirit recognized Jesus as "the Holy One of God." Why did Jesus not need them to distinguish him? Likely on account of the feelings of trepidation and superstitions of the group.

Later on, Jesus was blamed for being allied with the devil (cf. Mark 3:22). He knew the opposition that would come, so maybe his command here is a direct result of that coming conflict.

Conclusion: Jesus Christ showed his power over every sort of evil. The Bible unmistakably shows that evil is close to home (personal), that it is Satanic, that it isn't just an impact, a conceptual thought. Evil is genuine, it's real. In these verses, we have seen evil as the satanic, the form of demonic and demon possession.

We have noticed the developing enthusiasm for the occult, maybe one of the most clear signs of the demonic. The most exceedingly awful, obviously, is simply the worship of Satan himself. It is difficult to envision, however in our very own day young people have actually been sacrificed to Satan.

Be that as it may, without being demon-possessed, people are likewise torn by different shades of evil of the day; depression, suicide, drug abuse, liquor abuse. This is a moderation exercise; these are subjects of indispensable concern. Evil takes its toll in numerous forms.

Sadly, in the past it has been said that liquor abuse, for instance, is a "demon." In the strict sense, this isn't valid. Evil spirits or demons are real spirit beings. Liquor abuse doesn't emerge out of demon possession. Obviously, it is an awful evil; so is any sort of illicit drug uses. Yet, by accusing these shades of evils on demons, we now and again get the feeling that people themselves are not responsible.

Liquor abuse originates from an assortment of causes: loneliness, nervousness, anxiety, sexual yearnings, issues at home, at work, etc. We are not being useful to people if we say it's a demonic presence. There are numerous approaches to support drunkards, but the recuperating needs in the first place a personal acknowledgment of need. No foundation (institution) can support a heavy drinker except if the person in question is willing to come and confess, "I need help."

The spiritual measurement is a part of the healing. Jesus Christ is as yet accessible today for the person who is dependent on anything: cannabis, heroin, liquor, tobacco, or sedatives. For healing to take place, there must be Christian love and compassion and the sharing of the power of Jesus Christ. There is no simple way out, when a person is oppressed (enslaved) to evil in any form.

We can't kick back and grumble about how horrendous conditions are on the planet. If Christians believe in Christ's power and love, they themselves must demonstrate it to the people who are suffering. Being enslaved to anything implies acute suffering of some kind. Self-control comes only through giving control of your life to Jesus Christ.

(Depict your own response, had you been a native of Capernaum. What might it take to get you amped up for Christ's power today? Identify some of the needs in the lives of neighbors and friends. Is there some way you can get them to meet Jesus?)

Chapter Ten

Power Over Sickness And Death
(Luke 7:11-23 NIV)

AILMENT AND DEATH ARE not aliens to us, in spite of the fact that we normally lean toward not to think about them. We live in a society that reveals opposing frames of mind: from one perspective, there has been a recovery of enthusiasm for good well-being (health), in healthy nourishments, in a healthy environment, then again, more people are drinking and smoking themselves into ill health and death than ever. Pleasure evidently precedes health for many people.

The Bible doesn't make a fixation out of good health, in spite of the fact that Christians are advised to deal with their bodies on the grounds that their bodies are the temple of the Holy Spirit. By and large, it appears, that great health is a by-product of obedience to the Bible's moral commands.

In any case, there is significantly increasingly more about sickness and death in the Bible than about how to be healthy. People who pursue the best spiritual and therapeutic (medical) counsel do become ill; we battle against those ills for which there is no known cure. As the messenger Paul noted, "Our outer nature is wasting away...the earthly tent we live in is destroyed" (II Cor. 4:16;5:1).

The Bible discloses to us how to confront this process; it tells to us how to experience the renewal of the inner man step by step, even while the external nature is decaying. The Bible discloses to us how to be of good courage.

The power we need over affliction (sickness) and death is nothing else but the power of the presence of Jesus Christ. His undergirding, fortifying (strengthening) presence is the thing that we need in the hours of agony (pain) and distress (sorrow). Jesus healed many people and raised some from the dead.

We can pray to God for healing today; we can express gratitude toward God for the miracles of current medicine. Be that as it may, when God's will is suffering and death, he gives us mental fortitude (courage) and faith to endure as we commit ourselves completely and fully to the love of Jesus Christ. His love and power are what we need to see in this lesson.

The Widow's Son Raised
(Luke 7:11-17 NIV)

This lesson isn't organized chronologically, but topically. We are not following the life of Jesus in historical sequence. This is the second in a series of five lessons on the unique authority of Jesus as it was shown in the lives of people he met.

In this lesson we study one of those chance gatherings. Jesus was making a trip starting with one place then onto the next and met a person in great need. This is the account of how he met that person's need and brought great glory to God. His compassion won the day.

The Funeral Procession
(vv. 11, 12)

For a significant part of the time Jesus headquartered in Capernaum on the Sea of Galilee, however he also made visits to different communities. For reasons unknown, on this event he chose to go to Nain, a community situated about a day's voyage toward the southwest.

Jesus was accompanied by his disciples and an excited horde of well-wishers. These people were following Jesus as a prevalent legend (a famous hero) and miracle worker. They found in him a way to get what they deeply desired; similarly not many of them understood and believed his spiritual demands.

While in transit to Nain this upbeat group experienced a funeral service parade leaving Nain to the burying ground outside the city. The complexity was evident as the two groups united: the one, brimming with high expectations and eagerness; the other, loaded with despondency, fear, and sorrow.

The tragedy was significantly progressively pointed on the grounds that the survivor was a widow, and she was burying her only son. She had experienced sorrow once before. Now she would be left alone, under the social pressure of being a childless widow.

There was no expectation for her, either in Jewish religion or culture. She would be left to carry her emotional and spiritual concerns and burden alone.

The custom was for a whole community to show up for the funeral service procession. Homes and organizations were covered. The expert musicians and grievers headed the gathering, trailed by the pallbearers with the coffin, at that point the family members, relatives, and finally the people of the town.

The Lord's Compassion
(v. 13)

Commonly the group originating from Capernaum would have yielded the way to the funeral service procession. You can envision how their talking would have stopped when they saw what was coming their direction. There was no motivation to get included; simply stop and let the funeral service pass by. Be that as it may, the Lord Jesus Christ would not stand by in quiet recognition of the custom. His eye caught a person in intense need, the sorrowing widow. His compassion for her was so strong to such an extent that he intruded the funeral service procession to speak with her.

This was unheard of. It was socially off-base to break in like that and it was also inconsiderate and provocative to speak with a strange woman.

Be that as it may, Jesus would not bow to social boundaries. He went up to the woman and advised her to quit crying. He tended to himself to her most squeezing pressing need: overpowering sorrow, harshness, despair, and maybe spiritual inquiries concerning the justice of God for her situation.

Might she be able to trust her ears? Is it true that someone was really addressing her, attempting to comfort her? Presumably she had never seen Jesus, in spite of the fact that she may have found out about him. Notwithstanding her bewilderment, the Lord Jesus would bring her encouraging comfort and strength.

Jesus takes a look at human needs and reacts with compassion. That is the reality each Christian must handle. This isn't where the person included had great faith.

The widow's only claim to the attention and consideration of Jesus was her need. Ailment (Sickness) and death had incurred significant damage, and she was left to continue by one way or another. By then Jesus entered her life.

Jesus willingly diverted normal duties and plans to practice his love. This shows what confidence we can have to bring our needs to him. When sickness and death threaten, we can call upon him; his line is rarely occupied, we don't get the answering service, we get Jesus himself.

Christ's compassion becomes the asset that transcends all human assistance. His love is directed to our particular need, because he thoroughly understands it. This enables the Christian to confront emergency crisis realistically, but not in his own strength alone.

Obviously, we will weep when friends and family are taken, and we will be concerned when genuine sickness threatens. But, to endure and to triumph over the conditions we should make fresh commitments to Jesus Christ, so that his love can sustain us.

The Lord's Power
(vv. 14, 15)

After telling the widow to stop crying, Jesus moved toward the open coffin and the bearers halted in absolute surprise. any contact with the dead was a definitive in strict and social sullying.

Such contact was encompassed with the most exceedingly awful feelings of trepidation. These feelings of trepidation depended on the Old Testament laws which still bound the people of Christ's day.

Be that as it may, tainting didn't dissuade Jesus. He really touched the coffin and addressed the cadaver (corpse). Is it safe to say that he was insane? At this point the horde of well-wishers from Capernaum, just as the grievers, were confused. They had never seen anything like this.

Incredibly, Jesus advised the corpse to get up and the dead man got up and started to speak. Such was the power of Jesus Christ over man's fear and enemy, death. This present man's need was genuine life, and Jesus offered it to him once more. Jesus showed in a real demonstration that he is Lord of the universe, the great, all-powerful Creator.

With another excellent case of delicacy and love, Jesus gave the dead youth ("young man," Jesus addressed him) back to his mother. He did this because she was in no emotional or intellectual condition to comprehend what was happening.

It had occurred so rapidly. In a second, as it were, the irreversible procedure of death had been turned around; the funeral service had become an event of new life rather than death. The broken up family had been put together; the bereaved widow had been given joy.

Right now Jesus demonstrated that he cares about sickness and death. Human misery, suffering and sorrow touched him deeply. His compassion invigorated his divine power.

Crossing the social and religious barriers, he found a way to go into the most profound needs of one obscure family. Their only claim on him was their need, giving full evidence to us today that we can take every one of our needs to Jesus.

Christian faith means trust in the Christ who cares. Jesus Christ cares not only about how we suffer emotionally and physically, but also how we suffer spiritually because of sin. The corpse in this incident speaks to physical death, but spiritual death also, in light of the fact that sin's greatest effect is spiritual death.

Every human being ever born physically is dead spiritually (cf. Eph. 2:1). Therefore, more important than physical life is spiritual life.

A person's most prominent need is not health but eternal life through personal faith in Jesus Christ. We will all die physically, but spiritual death can be defeated through the forgiveness and new life that Jesus gives. Jesus today raises spiritually dead people to life. That is the best miracle of all.

The People's Response
(vv. 16, 17)

No wonder fear held onto the crowd. How might you feel, if you would see a corpse getting up out of a coffin while you were at the funeral service? This was healthy fear within the sight of divine power. This is the correct kind of fear of God.

Be that as it may, at that point fear before long gave way to praise. The people glorified God because they knew he had been at work in their presence in the person of Jesus of Nazareth. They were witnesses to a miracle that only "a great prophet" could perform. They recognized the love and power of divinity in Jesus Christ, so they concluded that "God has visited his people."

This was their great expectation and hope, but they never expected to see a real resurrection. Be that as it may, they accepted the proof and they reached the correct conclusion. God was in Christ; he was revealing himself in an absolutely new way. Here was proof for faith and commitment.

Obviously, the news spread quickly. Would you be able to keep still in the event that you had seen a miracle such as this? be that as it may, regularly we neglect to praise God for what he accomplishes for us. Christians today haven't seen Jesus raise somebody from the dead, but consistently they receive endless physical and spiritual blessings. How would they spread the news that Jesus Christ really can save people from their sins?

Giving God the glory before one's companions and neighbors doesn't require miracles. If Jesus has done anything at all for you, that is something to share. Naturally, when he heals and provides a special need, we are more appreciative and bound to tell others. In any case, the Bible says we are to give thanks "in all circumstances" (I Thess. 5:18).

(Request that companions share what intrigues them most about Jesus on this event. Toward what kind of personal needs can the love for Jesus be communicated today? His power? What does it take to make his love and power genuine in personal involvement? How might you use this Bible episode to help somebody you know? What would Christians be able to do to prepare themselves spiritually ahead of time for sickness and death?)

John's Question
(Luke 7:18-23 KJV)

Here is an uncommon understanding (rare insight) into the life of John the baptizer, the one sent by God to set up the path for the ministry of Jesus Christ. John himself was giving witness to the way that Jesus was for sure God's sent one (cf. John 1:34).

He realized that he was the forerunner of the Messiah. Be that as it may, at some point after the people responded to John's ministry, John fell into hardship for upbraiding the king for taking his brother's wife. Thusly, Herod slapped him in jail (Luke 3:18-20). The question that comes to Jesus in these verses emerged out of John's prison experience.

Is Jesus The Messiah?
(vv. 18-20)

John's disciples clearly had access to his jail cell. They announced the superb things that Jesus had been doing. The most recent miracle was his raising up of the widow's son. This was such a stupendous occasion, that John had to know about it.

In any case, rather than rejoicing at the most recent news, John was troubled. His sureness about the recognize of Jesus as the Messiah for reasons unknown had disappeared while he was in jail. So he dispatched two of his disciples to put the inquiry legitimately to Jesus: "Would you say you are he who is come (i.e., the Messiah), or shall we search for another?"

For what reason was John currently experiencing such uncertainty? Forlorn hours in jail can accomplish abnormal things' to one's mind. Maybe clashing reports had arrived at his ears. Maybe he discovered a portion of his Messianic desires unfulfilled. John could have been trusting that Jesus would secure his release.

We can't make certain, obviously, but there is a suggested censure of his absence of conviction in verse 23. In spite of his concern as of now, John's stature was not decreased according to Jesus (cf. vv. 24-28).

John brought up the essential issue each person needs to raise: Who truly is Jesus of Nazareth? Christ's control over sickness and death is expected to assist us with finding the correct answer. His power was a indication of his deity, that he genuinely is God the Son, the God-man sent from heaven by the Father to redeem the lost race.

When we see Jesus Christ's love and power in real life we should gain knowledge into his character, so we will come to entrust ourselves and our eternal salvation to him. Truly, we will all have times of vulnerability, times of questions, particularly when difficulties assail us.

John was locked up, forbidden to preach. Often we are defeated by circumstances over which we have no control. At such times we need firm faith in who Jesus truly is.

The Evidence of Mighty Deeds
(vv. 21-23)

Jesus didn't address the inquiry presented by John's disciples straightforwardly. Would it be a good idea for him to have basically said truly, to dissipate the majority of John's questions? Was this roundabout strategy harder on John? Maybe it was, yet our Lord's answer must be established in some essential proof.

John needed to take a look at what Messiah should do, contrast that and what Jesus had done, and afterward arrive at his very own decision.

Along these lines, Jesus advised the men to answer to John what they had "seen and heard." John couldn't see with his own eyes, so he required the declaration of observers (witnesses).

Jesus gave six actualities to substantiate his case. His case to be the Messiah could be confirmed by the proof: the visually impaired (the blind), the faltering (the lame), the hard of hearing (the deaf), and the pariahs (lepers) were healed; the dead were raised; the poor heard the good news from his lips.

What more proof was vital? The appropriate response Jesus gave paralleled his perusing from Isaiah about the Messiah (cf. Luke 4:18, 19). Jesus was doing what the Old Testament anticipated Messiah would do. So Christ's activities saw to his relationship to God.

He was in excess of a conventional (ordinary) human being; he had unique power that enabled him to deal with the most noticeably terrible potential cases in the public arena. God, as it were, confirmed who Jesus was by these special manifestations of his power.

Jesus added a warning here (v. 23). It is conceivable to see the signs indicating his divinity, but then miss the way to salvation.

Seeing supernatural miracles isn't sufficient to save anybody. People must act on what they have seen and heard about Jesus Christ.

But numerous onlookers in Christ's time, and numerous who read a mind-blowing record today, disapprove of him. They state he was simply one more Jewish faith healer, a religious freak, a progressive, a good man, an unusual teacher, however he truly wasn't God in human flesh.

This is on the grounds that they would prefer not to grapple with his spiritual demands upon them, the demands that they repent, believe, and keep his commands.

So there are the onlookers who overlook what's really important, all things considered, Be that as it may, had you been among poor people, the visually impaired, and the sick healed by Jesus you would have had an alternate point of view.

When moved by his life and power, you would be a changed person. Today we face the same opportunity. Would we be able to encourage people to open themselves to Christ, whatever their needs?

There are incalculable opportunities to share Jesus Christ's love and power in word and deed. Frequently people won't accept our words of testimony until they see a few deeds of love and sacrifice. The two go hand in hand. Jesus preached to poor people, but he likewise healed them. "Is Jesus really the divine Savior?" people are inquiring. What proof do Christians bring to the table today?

(Ask companions for their thoughts regarding for what reason John had questions about Jesus. What causes questions in our lives? How might we strengthen our faith notwithstanding sickness and death? What proof do we need to take a look at? What signs do you see that people are searching for spiritual truth? For what reason is their search often covered up until some disaster strikes?)

End: How much proof does it take to make a believer? What more could God have done to persuade the world that Jesus was genuinely his fully divine Son? Christians attest that the proof is adequate, the record is clear enough to make a faith promise to Jesus Christ. However that commitment is tried and refined by the flames of difficulty, often by sickness and death. We need strong faith to address the difficulty. Jesus Christ won't fail us when we come to him in the time of need.)

Chapter Eleven

Jesus' Power To Forgives Sin
(Luke 7:36-50 NIV)

SOME PORTION OF THE disturbance and pressure in the present society never rises to the surface, it is kept contained inside people who are either unforgiving or unforgiven. From one perspective, there are people who have been wronged, but they can't force themselves to forgive the transgressor; then again, there are the people who know they have fouled up, yet they have never been forgiven by the one they offended.

Such shaky human connections cause the most noticeably awful sort of friction and misery: homes are divided; people don't converse with one another at work; neighbors will not be neighborly. In any case, what we find in human experience is just an impression of a similar issue on an a lot bigger scale, the issue of our offenses against God.

Be that as it may, scarcely any individuals are eager to begin at the root of the issue. They need to see social change, they want better human connections, but they would prefer not to examine the spiritual factors.

The Bible proclaims that we as a whole have offended God; we have gone our own specific way against his will; we have dismissed his initiative and guidance in our lives; we have abused his ethical (moral) commands; we have not done the good, the true, and the correct things we ought to have done. In this way, our relationship with God is out of kilter. Except if it is corrected, we face certain judgment.

What would we be able to do about this issue? God offers an exit from the spiritual predicament; he offers to forgive our offenses and our bad behavior. We can make things right with God by confessing our wrongs and accepting his forgiveness. When the divine-human level of relationships is fixed and cleansed, we can offer and accept forgiveness on the person-to-person level.

Our messed up human relationships should drive us to seek God's forgiveness. He can make us new people. This lesson shows how God acted in Jesus Christ to forgive sin. Be that as it may, unless people are aware of what sin is and does, they won't respond to Jesus Christ's forgiveness.

Christians need to be clear on both sides of the coin: the meaning of sin and the meaning and importance of forgiveness.

Jesus Anointed By A Sinner
(Luke 7:36-39 NIV)

The everyday grouping of events in Jesus Christ's life frequently brought unexpected open doors for spiritual teaching. Over and over he held onto these events to drive home significant truth. The fact of the matter was anything but difficult to find in these cases because it was being worked out in real life circumstances.

There was nothing hypothetical about his teaching on forgiveness. For this situation, an interrupted on evening gathering (dinner party) served to show the self-righteous Pharisees what forgiveness was about.

Dinner At The Pharisee's House
(v. 36)

The scene is the home of a wealthy Pharisee, Simon, most likely in Capernaum during the early part of Jesus Christ's Galilean ministry, A.D. 28-29. Jesus was welcome to dinner by Simon, who presumably wanted to take a direct look at the new prophet who who making great claims and performing miracles.

The Pharisees were the strict religious defenders of Israel; they were the strict keepers of the laws and the customs. They willingly volunteered to choose for the people what was right and what was wrong.

They had rejected John's baptism (v. 30) and were becoming progressively suspicious of Jesus. One reason was on the grounds that he associated with people they scorned socially and religiously.

Jesus was very much aware of their criticism of him (v. 34), yet he was not deterred by their narrowness and hypocrisy. He ate with the tax authorities and sinners and now he would eat with the Pharisee.

The Woman's Worship
(vv. 37, 38)

The woman isn't named, however she is distinguished as "a woman of the city, who was a sinner," which means she was an infamous whore. She discovered that Jesus was eating at Simon's home, so she chose to go there to exhibit her love for him. This she did by blessing his feet with salve (ointment) and with her tears.

It was phenomenal for excluded visitors to be found at a feast. The woman would effectively have the option to arrive at Jesus, on the grounds that the visitors leaned back on a love seat at the table. In this position their feet would be behind them.

Her aim was to spill out her costly aroma on the feet of Jesus, yet as she did so she was defeated emotionally. Most likely the salve had been paid for by her very own shameless profit. Provided that this is true, it spoke to a sacrifice of impressive cost, but it likewise meant the surrendering of her corrupt, sinful life.

The lavish showing of love was, obviously, startling and out of request for the event, however the woman was under an excess of enthusiastic worry to be disturbed by what people thought. Her love essentially flooded.

"She began to wet his feet with her tears" signifies "to water with a shower." Her tears poured down in a flood on the feet of Jesus. As she twisted down to kiss his feet, she cleaned them with the only towel she had, her hair. Regularly slaves washed their lord's feet with their very own hair.

The Pharisee's Objection
(v. 39)

Simon didn't stop the woman and he didn't dissent straightforwardly, however he was reaching a decision about Jesus. Was Jesus a prophet or not? How was the Pharisee to tell? He chose the premise of how Jesus responded to the prostitute's worship and love.

In the event that Jesus were a prophet, he figured, he would have rejected the woman and wouldn't have anything to do with her. Since Jesus didn't turn the woman aside, he should not be a prophet.

The general purpose of the Pharisee's judgment was contact with sinners. It was inconceivable to Simon that Jesus, was a holy man of God, would enable this woman of the street to touch him.

The Pharisees could be sullied by any social inclusion with Gentiles and known sinners. Their lives depended on cautious separation. They would go across the road to abstain from passing a sinner; they could never go into a Gentile's home. So deeply instilled was this way of thinking that Simon precluded Christ's case to be sent from God based on his relationship with the woman.

Dr. John Thomas Wylie

(In what ways do people attempt to look at Christ today? In what manner would Christians be able to be a means for helping people discover reality with regards to him? Do you think your non-Christian neighbor would be positively dazzled by your love of Jesus? What do you think it cost the woman to make her exhibition of love for Jesus? For what reason do the vast majority will in general be progressively repressed (inhibited)?)

The Principle Illustrated
(Luke 7:40-43 NIV)

Like Nathan the prophet with David the king, Jesus makes the spiritual rule unmistakable by methods for a basic story. He likewise forces Simon himself to articulate judgment working on it.

Jesus realized that Simon was humiliated by this unrestrained presentation of adoration from such a bothersome (undesirable) person. He realized that Simon was truly passing judgment on him based on false models, but Jesus didn't defend himself for this situation; he defended the woman and guided Simon toward the genuine significance of forgiveness.

The Lord's Question
(vv. 40-42)

With certainty and effortlessness Jesus tested Simon's grandiose demeanor. The story was perfectly clear. Two men were in the red (debt), one of them multiple (10xs) times worst than the other. (The denarius was about a homestead specialist's day by day pay, so the one man was under water for a sum equivalent to over year and a half's work.) But the man to whom the cash was owed forgives the two indebted individuals.

Maybe in this anecdote the individual with the obligation of 500 denarii spoke to the sinful woman and the man with the obligation of fifty denarii spoke to Simon. In any case, the end was the equivalent for them two; both were bankrupt and both were forgiven their debts.

At that point the Lord posed a clear inquiry: Which of these individuals would love the loan boss (creditor) more?

Simon's Answer
(v. 43)

Simon had to confront actualities (facts). It was maybe difficult for him to move, but there was no getting away from reality. So he turned out with the undeniable answer: the person who is forgiven the most will show the most love. Jesus complimented him for his answer.

The meal started with Simon attempting to make a judgment about the Lord Jesus. Now with this social interference, and with Simon's consequent wrong judgment about Jesus, he winds up being checked by Jesus.

This is the standard pattern of spiritual investigation. At the point when people investigate Jesus truly, they before long find that he places demands upon them. They need to respond to inquiries concerning themselves. Jesus drives us to take a look at ourselves sincerely. In the event that we neglect to do that, we will neither find the truth with regards to him nor the forgiveness we need.

(What attitude does Jesus show now in the incident? For what reason didn't he depend his conduct? For what reason does he center us around Simon instead of the woman? For what reason would it say it was not an embarrassment for Jesus to receive and accept the woman's affection?)

The Forgiven Sinner
(Luke 7:44-50 NIV)

Jesus turned from parable to the real world. The object of his lesson on forgiveness was a real individual. This was not religious hypothesis with Jesus, but the flesh and blood reality. Jesus never discussed something he couldn't demonstrate.

When we need to find our appropriate response to him, and how he treats us, we need only to take a look at real-life evidence. A lot of our disarray (confusion) and hesitation in spiritual issues could be cured if we would focus on the evidence of the real, but actual cases.

What The Woman Did For Jesus
(vv. 44-46)

"Do you see this woman?" Jesus asked Simon. Obviously he did. How might he abstain from seeing her? She was the person who intruded with an extraordinary showcase of worship. In any case, now the intruder becomes the object lesson. Jesus demanded that Simon observe her cautiously. "Take a look at her," Jesus says in actuality, "and you will understand what it means to be forgiven."

Dr. John Thomas Wylie

Simon would not like to take a look at the despised prostitute. None of us want to confront the dark realities of life. We prefer not to confront facts. In any case, at some point or another Jesus will make us take a look at sin. When we do, we need to settle on a decision either to proceed in sin, or to ask Jesus Christ's forgiveness.

Jesus didn't have to familiarize Simon with the woman's past; that was well known. But, he needed to familiarize Simon with her future and with the reason for the overflowing of her affection (love). When Simon could get a handle on why the prostitute had acted as she had, he would begin to understand what it means to be forgiven.

So directly Jesus made Simon take a look at the difference between his very own conduct and that of the uninvited guest. Simon has not been rude to Jesus; he had played out the obligations of friendliness and hospitality, but he had not gone out his way to give Jesus a special welcome. By contrast the sinful woman had lavished her commitment (her devotion) upon Jesus.

Note the difference: Simon gave Jesus no water for his feet (that would have been a unique compliment to guests), but the woman washed his feet with her tears. Simon didn't give Jesus the kiss of welcome (greeting), but the woman kissed his feet endlessly. Simon didn't anoint Jesus even with basic olive oil, but the woman anointed him with costly sweet-smelling balsam.

What Her Love Proved
(vv. 47, 48, 50)

We have to pursue the point cautiously here. In his story Jesus brought up the issue of which account holder (debtor) had the most love. In the real circumstance within reach, who demonstrated the most love to Jesus? Clearly, the woman had. Had Simon indicated any love whatsoever past normal conventions? None by any means.

In this way, Jesus closed, the woman's showcase of love demonstrated that she had been forgiven much. She broke into the evening gathering since she wanted to offer thanks for Jesus Christ's forgiveness. Her appreciation was unreserved as a result of the profundity of her sin.

The debtor who owed most was forgiven most and he loved the most. Simon was unconscious of the obligation of his sin; he demonstrated little love since he didn't have the foggiest idea what it meant to be forgiven much.

The woman was not forgiven on the grounds that she shed tears on the Lord's feet; she shed those tears of thankfulness and love since Jesus had forgiven her. She comprehended what forgiveness was on the grounds that she had experienced it against her very own dark, sinful roots.

Her indecency was incredible to such an extent that she was overwhelmed by the miracle of Jesus Christ's free forgiveness. This represented her unconstrained presentation of love and worshiped.

We don't have the foggiest idea when she had met Jesus prior, but we do know from what she did at the table that she had recently heard and received the good news of repentance and forgiveness from Jesus Christ. By his words he had brought conviction and afterward release and acquittal to her blameworthy, overwhelming heart.

From other stories we know how the duty tax collectors and sinners found in Jesus a genuine companion (v. 34). His compassion drew them to him. Maybe this woman had essentially responded to Christ's general invitation, "Come to me, all who labor and are heavy laden, and I will give you rest" (Matt. 11:28).

Notwithstanding the conditions, we know she set her own faith in Jesus Christ; this is the thing that saved her (v. 50). One of those anonymous people in the groups around Jesus, she had quite recently accepted his offer of forgiveness. She trusted him to be true and committed her life to him. She didn't have the advantage of an individual meeting, but when the opportunity emerged at Simon's home, she demonstrated the truth of her faith and her forgiveness.

As the occasion unfolded (transpired), we see her love for Jesus showed first as proof of her being forgiven by Jesus. In proper spiritual sequence, she had set her faith in Christ, she had been forgiven, and afterward she poured out her love to him.

The point for people today is clear: If we show no love for Jesus Christ, this demonstrates we haven't been forgiven; it demonstrates we haven't been sensible (realistic) and honest in confronting our sins. The person who has been overwhelmed by the awfulness of sin will find release and forgiveness from Jesus Christ. In the outflow of love to him we find the most assuring words of all, "Your sins are forgiven."

Those are the words everybody needs to hear, both those whose sins may be in the classification of prostitution and those whose sins are "covered" by a respectable veneer. If Jesus never speaks those words to us, we have no expectation (hope) of heaven and everlasting life. If we are not forgiven by him, we will spend time everlasting in hell under the judgment of (and condemnation) of God.

There are only two classes of people: forgiven sinners and unforgiven sinners. In this woman's story we have strong proof that anybody can find forgiveness from Jesus Christ. It isn't difficult, but it's easy to do as such; it's anything but a mysterious religious methodology.

Fortunately, whenever and whatever place in our lives we can lay hold on the love for Jesus Christ. He died the cross and rose again to demonstrate his love for us, to demonstrate that sinners can be forgiven. They can be forgiven in light of the fact that Jesus took upon himself the just judgment and condemnation of everyone's sins.

To be forgiven, a person need only say, "I am a sinner. Jesus died for my sins. I accept his death for my sake (on my behalf). I confess my sins and ask that he forgive me." When that transaction takes place by faith, the sense of release will be so great that we also will want to shower Jesus tears and kisses of gratitude.

The Response Of The Guests
(v. 49)

The guests thought and wondered how any man could forgive someone else's sins. They had not yet landed at the correct solution to their inquiry, "Who is this man?" If they had known the appropriate response, they would have understood Christ's power to forgive.

Jesus has the power to forgive sins by virtue of his deity - he is God the Son - and by virtue of his atoning death. The apostle Paul confronted the inquiry: "Who is to condemn (us for our sins)?" His answer: "It is Christ Jesus who died, yes, who was raised from the dead" (Rom.8:34). There is no condemnation for sins if we have received Christ's death and resurrection by faith.

To find forgiveness, then, we should recognize two things: (1) our own transgression (sins), and (2) Christ's power and willingness to forgive us. The two realities include the message Christians need to impart to a universe of unforgiven and unforgiving people.

(Get some information about how they have demonstrated their love for Christ. How is it over the typical customs, as it were? By what means would Christians be able to keep a fresh touch of devotion to Jesus Christ for his having forgiven them? What might this say to other people who wonder about Jesus Christ?)

Simon and the woman and the two indebted people show that in spite of the fact that there are degrees of blame (guilt); or bankruptcy, or failure to wipe out the disrespect, and dishonor done to God, all people remain needing forgiveness. That is their only hope. When persuaded of their need, people need to respond to the inquiry raised by the dinner guests, "Who is this man?" By claiming the power and position to forgive sins, Jesus Christ was either a cursing trickster (blaspheming deceiver) (as the Pharisees thought), or he is God manifest in the flesh.

Chapter Twelve

Jesus Transforms Life
(Luke 19:1-10; Mark 8:34-36 KJV)

THE DYNAMICS OF CHANGE have since quite a while ago interested psychological analysts. What makes an individual change? Social change is anticipated on the possibility that people can be molded to change.

For instance, it was felt that the government's battle years prior, against well-being dangers of smoking was making huge progress for various years. The counter smoking ads appeared to have convinced many people to quit smoking.

Be that as it may, at that point the law was passed against cigarette ads on TV. When those ads stopped, so did the counter smoking plugs. From that point forward there has been a calculable increment in smoking.

The entire field of behaviorism depends on the possibility that people can be molded to change. The behaviorists sees research center animals being molded by rewards and punishments, so he feels that similar standards apply to human beings.

The Bible doesn't discuss mental molding (we call it psychological conditioning), it discusses Christ producing a new race of individuals - transformed individuals, a new creation. The new man in Christ is produced by the regeneration of the Holy Spirit (John 3:1-8). In the event that an person isn't conceived of the Spirit, he isn't changed.

Obviously, we as a whole become familiar with certain social qualities by outer molding. A child figures out how to avoid the hot stove by touching it one time. Be that as it may, the person who is genuinely changed from the back to front isn't simply molded by experimentation, by rewards and punishments.

The new man in the Bible is absolutely new in light of the fact that Jesus Christ lives in him. He experiences new life, spiritual life, eternal life. The substance of that life is the indwelling Christ. This is something no behaviorist can account for. It is undeniably more than mental molding.

In this lesson we meet a transformed person, Zacchaeus. We additionally become familiar with the conditions Jesus Christ set down for acquiring the transformed life.

The Curious Tax Collector
(Luke 19:1-5 KJV)

This unusual episode happened as Jesus was concluding his ministry in Peraea (around three and a half months, A.D 29-30) and heading for Jerusalem and the climatic occasions of Holy Week.

Once more, it tells us how much Jesus was keen or interested in people. Similarly as he searched out the grieving widow of Nain, so here he searches out an inquisitive tax collector. The experiences of Jesus with people are most enlightening and empowering. We realize what he was like and we are assured that he is interested on every last one of us.

Zacchaeus Identified
(vv. 1, 2)

Zacchaeus was a rich assessment gatherer (tax collector) who lived in Jericho, a city around seventeen miles east of Jerusalem. It lay in the lower regions (foothills) on the fundamental street from the Jordan River east toward Jerusalem. From that point on it was all tough to the capital.

Jesus took this direct route from Peraea east of the Jordan, crossed the waterway, and took the street fives miles further to Jericho, a flourishing, significant city. One of its main residents was Zacchaeus, depicted as "chief tax collector, and rich." This implies he gathered assessments for the Jews' Roman overlords. Expense (tax) collectors paid for the benefit and were permitted free hand in imposing charges and customs obligations.

Obviously, Zacchaeus was the leader of this branch of the Roman government in Jericho. Throughout the years he had collected impressive riches through his office. It was commonly acknowledged that such men filled their pockets illicitly by blackmail and by over the top assessment rates. The expense tax collectors were all around detested by the Jews and classed as sinners (v. 7), since they had sold out to the Romans and as a result of their not ill-gotten wealth.

Zacchaeus Effort To See Jesus
(vv. 3, 4)

Jesus was simply going through the city, however his appearance mixed a lot of disturbance (commotion). For a long time (three years) he had been teaching and working miracles. While in transit to Jericho he had restored a visually impaired (blind) man's sight (1'8:35-43). Normally the roads would be thronged.

Among the inquisitive spectators was Zacchaeus, who most likely wasn't accustomed to bumping with the groups in the roads. Be that as it may, in spite of his riches and position, he didn't have a ringside seat to the parade.

He needed to battle for a spot to see, but he was blocked in light of the fact that he was pretty much nothing. In a shaking crowd there was no way for him. So he took to a tree along the road.

The sycamore dislike our sycamore trees. It was a fig-mulberry; its natural fruit was figlike, however its leaves were like those of the mulberry. Its curious method for developing with enormous branches abominable and all the way open made it a simple 'matter for Zacchaeus to move into it and out over the road.

For what reason would he say he was so decided "to see what Jesus' identity was"? Presumably on the grounds that he needed to see the man who had a notoriety for being well disposed with those whom the people everywhere loathed. He was something beyond another tourist; he gave off an impression of being keen on discovering exactly what sort of person Jesus was.

Maybe Zacchaeus had even caught wind of Levi (Matthew) the previous tax collector at Capernaum who had left his place of employment to turn into a full-time disciple of Jesus.

Zacchaeus wasn't taken to Jesus by companions, nor did he have a quick issue that required the Savior's consideration. He searched out Christ absolutely on his own initiative, and he defeated genuine impediments to get his firsthand look.

Jesus Invited Himself
(v. 5)

Most likely Zacchaeus felt silly roosted in the tree. He couldn't get away from the notice of the crowd and likely was the butt of sneers and hatred. Be that as it may, he endured and his industriousness was compensated by Jesus.

Zacchaeus just needed to get a good look at this celebrated individual, however he got considerably more than that. Jesus halted straightforwardly under the tree and called Zacchaeus by name. Not only that, he welcomed himself to be the visitor of this detested tax collector.

This, obviously, was an incredible thing. Jericho was the sensible spot for Jesus to stop for the afternoon, preceding making the long move into Jerusalem. In any case, nobody in the city offered him neighborliness (hospitality). So he picked the home of Zachaeus.

This was the start of an emotional defining moment in his life. Zacchaeus would now have the chance to have the Messiah as his very own home guest. The searcher was really the discoverer for this situation.

We have no other record of Jesus accomplishing something like this. He had on different events been welcomed into homes. His notoriety was spread by some who called him "the companion of tax collectors and sinners."

He likewise welcomed himself since he could comprehend the heart of Zacchaeus. This was in excess of a social call, as we will see. At the point when Jesus comes our direction, he needs to bring new life.

(Ask allies to share for what valid reason they think Zacchaeus was so resolved to see Jesus. For what reason did Jesus pick this present man's home for rest and refreshment, when he could have remained with a portion of the "good" people of the city? What spurs people today "to see what Jesus' identity was"? How does Christ make his presence known today? What job do Christians play in this?)

The Converted Tax Collector
(Luke 19:6-10 KJV)

All of a sudden life took an entirely unexpected turn for Zacchaeus. Rather than being an obscure face in the group, he turned into the focal point of consideration. He needed to settle on a brief moment choice.

We can't foresee the manners by which God will come to us; we can't make even our very own decisions; they are constrained upon us by conditions. The way in to the changed life is settling on the correct decision at the opportune time. This is the thing that Zacchaeus did.

The Joyful Reception
(v. 6)

Abruptly the parade halted and Zacchaeus was presented with a summons to act rapidly. What would it be advisable for him to do? There was no time for discussion or insight. He needed to say either, "Sorry, Jesus, you can't come today," or, "Truly, Jesus please come and go right ahead."

Zacchaeus chose to invite Jesus, and he did it rapidly. The fervor of the magnificent open door held him; presently he could truly discover what Jesus was like, from a tree as well as right in his very own home. Sheer pleasure at the possibility of this individual experience made him react. He got Christ "euphorically."

This was a delightful picture of trusting in Christ by faith today. Not every person needs to make such a speedy, on-the-spot decision, but when the call of God comes we do need to choose one way or the other.

Zacchaeus followed up based on earlier data. He knew something about Christ from a distance, but he needed to make that information personal. The initial step was to open his home to Christ; the second was to open his life to him.

Saving faith that delivers the transformed life (changed life) starts with learning about Christ - what his identity is, the thing that he has done, and what he can do. This knowledge is trailed by the responsibility of one's will to Christ, accepting him into one's life by a specific decision, for example, Zacchaeus had to make. That is the thing that we call conversion.

The Murmuring Observers
(v. 7)

The crowd despised the Lord's plan to remain with Zacchaeus. According to their own vain-glorious, self-righteous benchmarks, he had submitted a social and religious blunder. How could as far as anyone knows a holy righteous man pollute (defile) himself in such a manner?

There was no space for love, concern, and acceptance in their reasoning. Sinners were to be kept out, not invited in. A similar frame of mind taints some church people today.

The Proof Of Conversion
(v. 8)

We don't have the foggiest idea what words unfolded among Jesus and Zacchaeus while in transit to his home, which was presumably on the edges of Jericho where the wealthier people lived. We don't know precisely what produced this response in Zacchaeus, however what a colossal reaction it was.

His promise to Christ was demonstrated by what he offered to do with his cash. Genuine transformation will be trailed by deeds of righteousness. The transformed life isn't a life of sterile consideration, but a life of enthusiastic action. Change of heart will be seen by change of conduct.

Here is sensational proof of the power of Jesus to transform people. Zacchaeus vowed to give a large portion of his goods to poor people. His liberality far surpassed that of the double-dealing, pretentious Pharisees who prided themselves on multiplying the tithe and giving a fifth for help.

Further, he offered to make compensation to anybody he may have cheated. Restitution, but by four fold the amount. He didn't really implicate himself as an extortioner, however it was commonly acknowledged this is the thing that tax collectors did, so he was prepared to go a long ways past what was relied upon to make things right.

The Salvation Of The Lost
(vv. 9, 10)

Out of this response to Christ came salvation. Jesus saw the proof of genuine spiritual renewal. He articulated that one of "the lost sheep of the house of Israel" had been found. Zacchaeus, a son of Abraham by race, was presently a child of Abraham by faith as well.

Zacchaeus wasn't saved by giving ceaselessly his cash; his liberality was the product of the change that had been fashioned in his heart. He was another man, Jesus saw the proof, and pronounced him to be among the saved.

This episode filled to represent the need of Christ's coming. Here was verification of what his crucial: "to look for and to save" the lost. He had searched out Zacchaeus in the tree and he had saved him by the power of his own presence.

Zacchaeus had been "lost" as in he had discovered no importance throughout everyday life; he had no personal relationship with God; he was simply attempting to collect riches. At the point when he was saved, or found, his whole life focus changed. In the person of Christ he had met the living God, and that was a transforming experience.

The lostness of people is seen strikingly surrounding us today. The lost don't have the foggiest idea where they are going now, and they are uncertain about everlasting life. If they don't go to Christ, they will be lost until the end of time. The Christian offers a seeking for Christ who has power to find, to save, and to transform.

(Request that a companion propose to a potential discussion among Jesus and Zaccheus. What was Zaccheus' most prominent need throughout everyday life? How did Jesus meet it? How did this rich man enter the kingdom? Request that another examination part share what changes Jesus realized when they welcomed him into their lives. Are there yet any progressions to be made? How would you represent this emotional turnaround in the life of Zacchaeus?)

The Cost Of Discipleship
(Mark 8:34-36 NIV)

In these verses Jesus clarifies the exact condition of Christian discipleship. His portrayal is general, with the goal that every believer should work out the implications. The way of life that he pictures for a Christian is so unique in relation to the accepted qualities and guidelines of the world, that it can come about only by spiritual change. It's anything but a matter of outer regimentation, but of inward renewal - something that Jesus Christ in the believer must achieve.

The Call To Follow Christ
(v. 34)

Self-denial is the essence of discipleship and the transformed life. Jesus depicted it as far as taking up a cross and following him. For this situation, the cross isn't a burden to bear, however an instrument of death to self.

The cross Jesus discussed was a well-known sight along Palestinian streets. The Romans hung their unfortunate casualties (victims) there to caution would-be rebels.

Hence, self-denial means accepting the death penalty for one's own will and desires. Jesus didn't determine what it is that his followers ought to deny themselves. In any case, he said that the cross must be taken and applied. Without the cross, there is no denial of self.

Self can speak to the old nature, the basic sin nature, the unrepentant, unregenerate heart. Self wants to do whatever it wants, whatever will fulfill some flashing objective, regardless of whether it be cash, sex, notoriety, prestige, work headway, the most recent devices and recreational equipment.

When a person becomes a Christian and follows Christ, the old desires are transformed; they are supplanted by new spiritual desires. This is the positive side. "Follow me," Jesus stated, "rather than your old narrow minded nature." That is the decision to be made. Nobody can have it the two different ways. If self is standing out in the way, you can't follow Jesus Christ. Jesus demands total allegiance, total faithfulness.

The Choice To Be Made
(v. 35)

Here is a paradoxical statement. If at last we attempt to save our lives (that is, the desires of the old self), we will lose what we are attempting to save. In any case, in the event that you accept the cross as an instrument of death to yourself ("lose your life"), you will at last save your life. This is totally conflicting to the world's perspective.

The world's wisdom says we ought to do all that we can to excel, to be someone, to amass riches, to entertain ourselves. In any case, Jesus said that is the best approach to lose everything. Much better to deny what self needs and acknowledge rather the lordship of Jesus Christ. His control truly signifies "losing my life" for his sake, but that is the only way I can truly save it.

The Priority Of Spiritual Life
(v. 36)

What is genuine (real) life worth? For some people, life is just picking up as much out of each understanding and open door as they can. They need fulfillment, joy, and security. They will make due with not exactly the entire world, however at any rate they need something.

In any case, Jesus said there is a higher need; indeed, nothing outperforms the estimation of genuine spiritual life, eternal life. In this way, don't enable some other objectives to make you "relinquish" this reality. You need to deny yourself to pick it up, however it is justified, despite all the trouble.

This sort of life comes when Jesus does his changing work. He offers undeniably more than the world. Following him is the most fulfilling life there is.

(For what reason is it difficult to deny yourself? For what reason is it harder to pursue Jesus Christ than to acknowledge the world's qualities? How might an individual's life be changed if the followed Jesus Christ's states of discipleship?)

End: Values and attitudes are difficult to change. We are molded by numerous impacts. The Christian is molded by the control of Jesus Christ; truth be told, he is being made like Christ (Rom. 8:29). Jesus Christ is the overwhelming change operator in his life. The Christian faith doesn't urge people to change; the Christian faith says, "Let Christ change you. At that point you will locate the genuine importance of life."

Chapter Thirteen

Religion Can Be Vital (Power
For Creative Living)
(Mark2:23-3:6 KJV)

WHAT IS CREATIVE LIVING? Is it "accomplishing
your very own thing"? That is a well known idea
today. People need to be out from under rules and
guidelines. They say, "Let me do however I see fit,
long as I don't hurt any other person."

God gave humanity free moral choice,
basically, to do however he sees fit. Nobody needs
to be a robot. In any case, there is an spiritual law
at work which decides that we should live with
the outcomes (consequences) of our decisions.

The outcomes are in some cases hard to
confront. All things considered, many people
figure they can find happiness and fulfillment
(satisfaction) by doing anything they desire to do.
In one sense, people get training, education and
take a stab at better employments to excel, so they
can be allowed to entertain themselves.

For a few, that implies spending their check in a bar on Friday night; for other people, it means placing their cash into a workmanship accumulation and afterward giving it to a historical center. There are numerous different potential outcomes between those two constraints.

One explanation people state they would prefer not to pursue any religion is on the grounds that to them all religion likens to rules and guidelines. To them, that is extremely uncreative. They would prefer not to be bound by moral and ceremonial laws. God to them is much the same as a mean elderly person, always edging you in.

It would appear superficially that it is difficult to be both devout and innovative (creative). Be that as it may, such an end forgets about the Creator, the person who makes creative living conceivable. There are no restrictions to what a person can achieve under the bearing of God's creativity.

The Christian message is this: Surrender your desires to Jesus Christ and he will free you from yourself to be really creative. Obviously, God has commands to be obeyed, but the genuine purpose for obedience is to please him and to find that he can make substantially more of you than you can make of yourself, regardless of what number of points of interest you may have.

In this lesson we find how the Lord Jesus Christ looked to teach the creative of love against a foundation of harsh standards. He was the most creative person who at any point lived, and we would do well to follow his way of life.

The Controversy In The Grainfields
(Mark 2:23-28 NIV)

This incident happened during the initial five months of Jesus Christ's ministry in Galilee (A.D. 27-28). After his first preaching visit, he experienced expanding restriction and antagonistic vibe from the scribes and Pharisees.

They were particularly delicate about what he did on the sabbath (cf. John 5:1-47 for a full exchange among Jesus and his faultfinders on the issue of healing on the sabbath).

The debate in the grainfields is accounted for by Matthew, Mark, and Luke. It represents the collision between the values Jesus was teaching and exemplifying and those of the old-guard traditionalists.

They were not prepared for anybody to step over the limits they had laid down. Jesus forced the issue and demonstrated how obedience to God involves following all of his precepts, not simply certain ones that had been explained on out of extent to the others.

The Disciples Gathered Grain On The Sabbath
(v. 23)

We know that it was Christ's custom to take part in the customary synagogue services on the sabbath day (Luke 4:16). It appears to be strange at to find him with his disciples in a grainfield on this day.

The appropriate response is that they lived off the land a significant part of the time. They had companions who offered them accommodation, however for reasons unknown nobody offered them a feast on this specific day. In this way, lunch needed to originate from what they could assemble en route.

Peter said on one occasion, "Lo, we have left our homes and followed you" (Luke 18:28). Grabbing what was left over in the grainfields was a part of the price these men had to pay to follow Jesus. Frequently, our most noteworthy chances to be creative for Jesus Christ emerge out of such predicament. When everything is given to us on a platter, there is no motivator, no incentive to be creative.

The Pharisees Accused The Disciples of Sabbath-Breaking (v. 24)

This time, be that as it may, rummaging got Jesus and his disciples in a tough situation with the religious authorities, the Pharisees, a gathering that painstakingly controlled all parts of religious and social behavior. Their idea of law included both religious and common law. To them this was an infringement of God's commands and an infringement of the laws they had forced on Jewish society.

The Old Testament law indicated that no gathering was to be done on the sabbath (Exod. 34:21). The Pharisees, clearly out to demonstrate that Jesus was a strict fake (a phoney), extended the law now, since what the disciples were doing was not harvesting. Truly, the law allowed gathering food in cases of need.

In any case, the Pharisees couldn't face anybody's breaking down their own interpretation. They chose what was good and bad in these cases. Along these lines the stage was set for a conflict among them and Jesus, a genuine issue since Jesus claimed he had originated from God. For this situation, settled in religious authority exceeded itself and Jesus accepted the challenge.

Jesus Defended His Disciples
(vv. 25, 26)

Jesus safeguarded (defended) one "unlawful" act by helping the Pharisees to remember another "unlawful" act performed by the incomparable King David. This isn't an instance of two wrongs making one right. We have to remember that the Pharisees had misinterpreted the case by disregarding another standard - the principle of need. They couldn't permit any special cases, yet Jesus demonstrated there were essential exemptions.

The key purpose of Jesus' response to the Pharisees' charge is that David and his men were "in need and...hungry." Because of those special conditions, David and his men are bread that the law said was to be eaten distinctly by the priests. Carefully, this was in opposition to the law, yet another rule was legitimate for this situation - the need of David and his men for something to eat.

Along these lines, as a result, Jesus addressed that his men were hungry, as well, so they reserved each option to assemble grain to eat on the sabbath. Jesus didn't urge his men to violate the law basically in light of the fact that they needed "to accomplish their own thing."

This was not an instance of choosing what to obey and what to ignore; it was anything but an instance of complying with a law because they didn't care for it. Knowing how the Pharisees had made their laws more inflexible (more rigid) than God had intended, Jesus attempted to assist them with enlarging their comprehension and to be progressively creative in their use of the essential standards of the law.

God isn't keen on perceiving how restrictive he can be; God desires freedom with restriction. Genuine freedom doesn't mean the non-attendance of any restrictions whatsoever; genuine freedom is accepting God's will and allowing him to make you more liberated (freer) than you could be by yourself.

Jesus Is Lord Of The Sabbath
(vv. 27, 28)

Jesus was not inspired by simply refuting the Pharisees and his disciples right. He needed to get at the root thought of the issue, which was authoritatianism of the most noticeably awful kind. The Pharisees perceived God as their authority, yet they went past his power and would not permit other undeniable standards to become possibly the most important factor. There was no space for different understandings in their plan of reasoning.

Jesus returned them to the premise of their sabbath-keeping limitations, the fourth commandment. The sabbath was established in God's creation work and rest. It is obvious from Exodus 20:8-11 that the sabbath was planned to benefit man - not to oppress him - on the day when he did no work. consequently, Jesus revealed to them they needed to get the correct point of view on their traditions, the principles they had added to the essential precept.

God didn't make humanity just so individuals could satisfy the law of taking off one day in seven. Or maybe, the polar opposite. He arranged the day for man's prosperity. The Pharisees had raised the day itself over every single other thought. They made people captives of the day.

It would have been exceedingly hard for anybody in Christ's time to be creative about sabbath-keeping. People were bound by custom. Today is anything but difficult to fall into this snare. Religion moves toward becoming obligation as opposed to joyful articulation.

Going to church is something you need to do on the grounds that it's Sunday. Providing for the work of God progresses toward becoming something like a church tax. In any case, God didn't plan that we should express our faith in dull, dismal schedules. There is plentiful space for better approaches for conducting worship, for new thoughts regarding how to serve and love people.

Is it true that we are stating then that there are no limits, no restrictions? Not at all. Jesus Christ himself is our guide; he "is lord even of the sabbath." That was a stunning explanation, since sabbath-keeping was the foundation of Jewish religion. Would anything be able to or anybody be incomparable over the sabbath itself? Jesus said he was.

Jesus didn't build up his own need over the sabbath so he may have all the earmarks of being exempt from the rules that everyone else follows moral demands. He kept and fulfilled the morality of the law in each regard. He was not a progressive culprit or a revolutionary lawbreaker, but he taught and lived out the highest principles and values of morality and ethics. In this he becomes the Christian's guide and example.

In actuality, if Jesus is lord of the sabbath he is master of everything. Obedience to him is the Christian's outperforming duty. The Christian life is a duty, not a free-wheeling undertaking. We are advised to keep Christ's commands (John 14:21, 23). We can't play reckless with his words.

In any case, this is not to duplicate the negative way of life portrayed by the Pharisees. Such an absolutely negative methodology - what you can't do - overlooks what's really important of wholesome, creative faith. Of course, there are negative directions - the "thou shalt nots" of the ten commandments, for instance - but that isn't the end of the issue.

The creative Christian will want to ask God, "How might I express my faith and obedience in new and energizing manners? How might I go ahead past what the vast majority acknowledge as normal Christian living? Is there some mentality that should be changed from negative to positive?"

The announcement, "Jesus is lord even of... allows us to incorporate anything in our lives. If there is something he isn't lord of, we are passing up on our more prominent open door for creative Christian living. At the point when he progresses toward becoming lord, he opens completely new regions of service and fulfillment. This is on the grounds that he is living and wise, and he knows how to build up the most out of our potential.

(Request that friends propose a few customs they feel are restricting them. Is it simple or troublesome in your church to present new thoughts? What is the wellspring of authority in your congregation? In your home? How can one keep up a feeling of duty and obedience to God's laws with a mentality of love? For what reason does keeping God's laws move toward becoming drudgery as opposed to creative to certain people? How might we animate each other to obey Christ as lord superior to anything we have previously?)

The Controversy In The Synagogue
(Mark 3:1-6 NASB)

The scene shifts from the grainfields to the synagogue, presumably at Capernaum (cf. 2:1). but, the heroes are the equivalent; the Pharisees are as still laying snares (traps) for Jesus.

This time, in any case, the purpose of dispute is the healing of a man with a wilted hand. In any case, underneath is a similar issue; sabbath-keeping and the negligent use of the standards related with it.

The Pharisees Waited To Accuse Jesus
(vv. 1, 2)

The Pharisees knew that Jesus was inspired and actuated by human need. This was not their inspiration; their inspiration was to tie down adjustment to rules and guidelines. So the stage was set for another showdown when Jesus experienced a man with a wilthered hand in the synagogue on the sabbath.

Would Jesus accept the challenge? Would he so to speak be creative enough to satisfy the greater levels of popularity of love and human need? If he did what was unlawful as indicated by the Pharisees, they would have a body of evidence against him.

They were not keen on perceiving how he interpreted and fulfilled the law; they only wanted to blame him for lawbreaking. It involved fundamental point of view on life and religion. Any deviation from the accepted routine was cause for being accused of lawbreaking.

Jesus Questioned Them About Doing Good On The Sabbath (vv. 3, 4)

In the wake of welcoming the disabled (withered) man to come to him, Jesus asked the Pharisees an inquiry. In this he pursued his standard method for compelling them to look at their off-base suspicions and ends.

The inquiry was penetratingly basic and made the issue completely clear. Could an individual really do good on the sabbath and be denounced for it? The Pharisees had been so far expelled from the equitable standards of the law that they said it wasn't right to do demonstrations of benevolence (mercy) on the sabbath.

To mend (heal) a man on the sabbath, they finished up was work. Since work was not permitted on the sabbath, healing the man would not be right.

This is a case of how one can begin with a right religious certainty and turn out with a wrong viable end. A day of rest was the sabbath rule, yet the guideline must be applied in accordance with the necessities of individuals. Their needs were significant and they couldn't be dismissed out of a craving to keep away from work.

In the grainfields, the followers were hungry and required nourishment; in the synagogue, a man needed to be healed. The Lord Jesus Christ couldn't acknowledge the impediments of preposterous human customs.

He likewise needed the people everywhere, who were helpless before the Pharisees, to see that a person could be dedicated to God and simultaneously not be enclosed by unnecessary limitations.

The Pharisees had no answer. They saw the rationale of Jesus and the deception of their reasoning. In actuality, Jesus showed this: "Not to do good, when it is in your grasp to do it, is underhanded (evil); not to save life, when you can, is to kill." Think of the creative ramifications of this teaching. Perceive how a long ways past the tolerant reasoning this standard goes.

As opposed to accept the base obligation, a Christian can be searching for approaches to do good, to save life, spiritually and physically. Jesus would appear to show that if we are not fulfilling our creative potential, we are resisting him and wrecking ourselves as well as other people.

Many Christians are substance to float along, keeping the apparent aim of the law. They don't consider making creative ventures for the master. They think little of their own potential. With Jesus in charge, anything can occur, the open doors for doing good are boundless. This is the test to our faith.

There is an unobtrusive test in his inquiry also, in light of the fact that Jesus knew the Pharisees were plotting to slaughter him. They conceded in their own laws that it was conceivable on the sabbath to offer help to a person whose life was in 'threat, and risk was translated generously. Then again, they were using the sabbath with dangerous aims. Which was increasingly suitable to the day, his recuperating or their plotting?

Jesus Healed The Man On The Sabbath
(v. 5)

Jesus was moved with love to heal the man, however he was enraged at the spiritual hardness of the Pharisees. This is one of only a handful hardly any entries that uncover our Lord's emotions. However even his exemplary annoyance was blended in with sadness. Spiritual hardness is dangerous, deadly and tragically people who are outwardly religious practically speaking frequently have cold, unbelieving hearts. They can't accept the freedom Jesus Christ offers.

The Pharisees Sought To Destroy Jesus
(v. 6)

This is the final product of cruelty. Jesus had come to show the method for God more impeccably than the composed code could, yet the Pharisees were held hostage by assumptions and traditions.

Ostensibly right, they missed the higher standards Jesus taught. They couldn't accept the new thing God was doing before their own eyes.

(Is Phariseeism a problem today? What is the response to it? In what manner can a Christian be creative? In what capacity can a Christian get new thoughts regarding love and service? For what reason do Christians now and then have the notoriety for being unchangeable and uncreative?)

End: In one sense, Jesus was the most creative person who at any point ever lived, yet he was totally faithful to his Father's will. Today obedience to God is as yet the way to power for creative living.

Jesus Christ makes his children new people (II Cor. 5:17 NASB). Christians are reestablished in knowledge after the image of God. With that huge potential, Why do we settle for anything short of the best God has for us?

Chapter Fourteen

The Way Of Unselfish Service
(Mark 10:35-45 KJV)

WE ARE RAISED TO be our very own man, as it were. We are instructed to be rough, intense people, cutting out our very own professions to excel, regardless of whether it means stomping all over others.

This is the reason Jesus Christ's teaching about unselfish service is so radical. His spiritual emphasis cuts across the accepted perspectives or views of life. We talk about social versatility social mobility), which means beginning at the base of the stepping stool, however in the long run we would like to have people working under us.

The gospel doesn't deny a person a chance to excel (get ahead), however it strikes at he childish frame of mind (being selfish) of using people as a means for communicating power. A person of riches (wealth) and position can be unselfish; the significant thought is one's intentions (motives).

Here is the place Jesus has such a great amount to say to us.

Whatever position God gives us throughout everyday life, whatever means he puts available to us, we can follow Jesus Christ's command to serve others. In this matter Christians ought to set the example for the world to follow. Unselfishness is a striking declaration to the power of the gospel to change people. When Christians essentially gorilla the world's frames of mind and thought processes, they are not representing Jesus Christ and his teaching fairly.

In this lesson we find how Jesus took care of a narrow minded move for power among his own disciples. They saw his kingdom in worldly terms of advancement and prestige, but he defined it as far as serving the needs and interests of other people.

The Request Of James And John
(Mark 10:35-37 KJV)

This episode happened as Jesus and the disciples were advancing toward Jerusalem once and for all. Peril and strain filled the air, expectations and fears mounted. The people realized how sharply opposed to Jesus the Pharisees were.

Jesus reliably encouraged that he would be killed by the religious leaders. Once more, as be started the climb by walking to Jerusalem, Jesus helped his disciples to remember his impending death and resurrection (10:32-34). It was in this atmosphere that James and John brought their request to Jesus.

The Sons Of Zebedee
(v. 35)

These two men got the sense of doom quickly drawing nearer, so they decided it was the time to make their move. They had been a part of Christ's inward circle on several occasions. Maybe they believed they had a corner on his favors. In any event, they felt more advantaged than the rest (cf. Mark 5:37; 9:2 KJV).

We may think they were excessively striking now (over boldness), yet clearly they felt close enough to Jesus to approach him secretly. He had taught them to confide in him and to live by faith. They had seen his mighty power displayed. Maybe they were in any event, thinking about his promise, "Ask, and it will be given you" (Matt. 7:7 RSV).

At any rate, we are appalled at the extent of their request: "We want you to do for us whatever we ask of you." Now they were interested not in the larger interests of the kingdom, but in what they could receive in return for themselves. This is an old style example of motives gone wrong. We are never urged to "use" God, in a manner of speaking, but rather to trust him to provide our basic needs.

Their Desire For The Chief Places In The Kingdom (vv. 36, 37)

Jesus welcomed them to proceed; he didn't give a straight yes or no now, despite the fact that he could have uncovered their narrow-minded selfishness right away. Frequently parents are placed in the equivalent cumbersome spot by their children. When they are approached to allow a limitless ticket to ride, in a manner of speaking, they generally answer. "Everything relies upon what you need."

Be that as it may, Jesus had at the top of the priority list a more spiritual lesson, so he permitted James and John to determine their request. They wanted to be at his right and his left when he accomplished his "glory." They perceived Jesus as king. The people who might be at his right and left would be in a favored position over the various subjects. They would be the king's central ministers. They would not be taking orders, they would give them.

Eventually, they needed power, prestige, and position. They were not searching for service. Out of twelve followers, some would have places over the others. It should be them. Additionally, they most likely wanted to get the edge on Peter, the third person from the inner circle, who frequently seemed, by all accounts, to be in a place of leadership among the twelve.

The request of James and John shows that they were persuaded of Christ's messiahship. They believed he had the power and authority to dispense the chief places in his glory. What they comprehended by "your glory," nonetheless, was a carefully political, gritty domain (an earthly domain) They anticipated the restoration of Israel's nationhood and the topple of the Romans. James and John notwithstanding Messiah's death were following the world's perspective.

Some way or another, they figured suffering may be avoided, for Jesus and for them. They didn't consider suffering to be the means by which Jesus would enter his glory. They wanted exaltation for themselves without suffering. "Glory" for them was getting a chief place. The essential spiritual elements of the kingdom eluded them now.

So the stage was set for the principal endeavored interest. It became out of wrong thought processes (wrong motives), misconception of Christ's mission, maybe also out of close to home and family contention. The mother of James and John was Salome, who appears to have been the sister of Christ's mother (15:40; Matt. 27:56; John 19:25).

Assuming this is the case, James and John would be first cousins to Jesus. Taken together, any of these realities can shield Christians today from practicing vital spiritual services. To put self first, as James and John did, takes out the best possible spiritual inspiration that is expected to serve others.

(Ask a companion to give their thoughts regarding for what valid reason James and John made this request of Jesus. What parallels show up today in church life? In home life? What makes "the chief place" so desirable? For what reason do you think James and John missed the implications of Christ's teaching in 10:32-34? Do you think some people today follow Christ for narrow-minded, selfish reasons? Show your answer.)

The Lord's Refusal
(Mark 10:38-40 KJV)

The Lord Jesus Christ conceded no private plans. He denied the solicitation, however clarified how far away base these men were in their reasoning. Every so often, as indicated by our restricted human shrewdness, we approach God for things we believe are for our good.

Frequently our solicitations are simply narrow minded (selfish). The Holy Spirit does a service of reproach at such occasions, and God arranges our conditions so that as opposed to giving us what we want, he gives us something better. For this situation, the "something better" was a new understanding of giving ourselves to other people.

Jesus Faced Them With Future Tests
(vv. 38, 39)

James and John thought glory would come at the snap of Christ's finger. They didn't foresee suffering, so Jesus corrected their misguided judgments on this point.

"You don't have the foggiest idea what you are asking means they were not aware of the cost of glory. Before any of Christ's servants could think about occupying a chief place in his kingdom, they would have to follow his example of suffering, his "cup" and his "baptism."

To "drink of a cup" is in Scripture a figure for getting one's fill of either good (Ps. 16:5; 23:5 116:13; Jer. 16:7), or of ill (Ps. 75:8; John 18:11; Rev. 14:10). Here is the cup of suffering. We understand baptism here in the allegorical sense, which means an immersion in overpowering sorrow.

This is the thing that lay in front of them; these tests would need to be faced before they were prepared to be Christ's chief assistants. The rule is that dignity and honor were earned, not given away as favors. Jesus pushed these men to consider the characteristics that must be displayed before glory could be presented. How capable would they say they were of the dignity which they yearned for?

How would we gain honor and prestige today? At times by family pedigree, by educational attainment, and by influence. It is entirely different in Christ's realm. It isn't who or what you know, however much you are prepared to suffer. The standard is by all accounts that he who is able to suffer most for Christ's sake will be nearest to him in his kingdom.

James and John certainly addressed that they were able to meet the tests of things to come. In the event that they had said no, they would have felt precluded. But then most likely they didn't question their own strength now. Theirs was not a fake answer, despite the fact that they couldn't now get a handle on the significance of it.

Unknowingly maybe, they offered the correct response, in light of the fact that in years to come they paid for their faithful witness to Christ with their lives. James was the first of the apostles to be baptized with his master's baptism of blood (Acts 12:1, 2 RSV). John endured the persecutions of the early church and partook in the suffering expedited by the advance of the gospel. After the others had gone to glory, he experienced his years (lived out his years) in harsh, bitter exile for the word of God and the testimony of Christ (Rev. 1:9).

Notwithstanding their shameful desire (unworthy ambition), these men remained true to Christ. Jesus was gentle with them; he didn't rebuke them now, because he knew what they would have to suffer for his sake.

The Chief Places Are Not Given As Favors (v. 40)

Jesus controls his administration not by bias (favoritism) however by fitness of character. James and John wanted the chief places as an outright favor. Jesus said they couldn't qualify on that premise; they may qualify on a similar premise as every other person. Selfish ambition and favoritism are the Lord's targets here.

The way is open for anybody to aspire to spiritual significance. The obligation goes to those whose hearts are in the right place. The Bible discussions about spiritual rule and authority growing out of obedience to Jesus Christ. Simultaneously, glory is promised to all who suffer with him (Rom. 8:17).

(Were James and John consequently ruled out of being at the Lord's right hand and left? Why or why not? For what reason couldn't Jesus promise them the chief places ahead of time? How is God testing your fitness for spiritual responsibility now? How is life a testing ground forever?)

The Key To True Greatness
(Mark 10:41-45 KJV)

Whatever the event, and in any event, when his disciples fizzled, Jesus drew out a spiritual application. What progressively fitting event to clarify what true greatness is! Two men needed to make a private bargain for a favored position, and Jesus tenderly and graciously transformed their request into a profound teaching.

Again we perceive how the values of Jesus were something contrary to the acknowledged perspective or the accepted way of thinking. The Christian must make similar value choices about his money, vocation, and position. It is difficult to pursue Christ's perspective here. Faith is required to obey him, in light of the fact that our human senses lead us the other way.

The Ten Were Indignant
(v. 41)

The solicitation for a favored position became exposed. The Lord's disciples were isolated; enmity created in the camp. Is it accurate to say that they were disturbed in light of the fact that their brothers had strayed spiritually, or would it say it was on the grounds that none of them wanted to be last?

Much of the time, when favoritism happens, the response is based on jealousy. No one wants to be passed over. This is a typical involvement in processing plants and workplaces. We by one way or another expect rivalry there. Be that as it may, we don't anticipate it among the disciples, nor among Christ's followers today.

One of the tests of our duty to Christ is the manner by which we respond to insults and dissatisfactions (slights and disappointments). It is difficult to be used, to be exploited, yet by one way or another Jesus doesn't anticipate that we should respond in the way of the ungodly. Here, the ten essentially followed their natural impulses.

Dr. John Thomas Wylie

The Example Of The Gentiles
(v. 42)

The disciples had heard Jesus teach about self-denial as the expense of discipleship. In any event once before they had contended about who was the best among them (9:34), and Jesus said they needed to become servants.

Presently he quietly goes over a similar ground once more. The stain of pride and prestige is hard to kill. The longing to be something is so profoundly ingrained.

This time Jesus indicated how the general public (society) of the world everywhere works. It's an extraordinary thing to rule over somebody, to practice authority over people. That is the acknowledged principle in the world. Jesus told his disciples the conspicuous truth in plainest terms with the goal that they may get a handle on the basic distinction between worldly greatness and spiritual greatness.

Men delight to domineer; they would prefer to be sergeants than privates. Men delight to use personal influence to secure private advancement. Now in their thinking about Christ's organization the disciples were simply following the world's examples.

The Priority Of Being A Servant-Slave
(vv. 43, 44)

"Be that as it may, "But" presents the major difference between Jesus and the world. The Christian walks to an alternate drummer, not the drummer of common notoriety and power but rather the drummer of servanthood.

"It shall not be so among you" features the distinction Jesus expected to see among his followers. They were to set an entirely unexpected standard. James and John got at risk with their solicitation, yet now the entirety of the men could see the differentiation between their reasoning and Jesus Christ's.

To be "great" and to be "first" are alluring objectives, however these objectives must be deciphered as Jesus did. That is the place Christians face genuine opposition. The great person is the servant, the person who positions initially is the slave. In Christ's order of things, genuine significance streams from lowly and voluntary help.

The suggestion is that spiritual authority grows out of the correct frame of mind (right attitude) toward self as well as other people. The "me first" frame of mind or attitude makes spiritual power outlandish. However even among the cooperation of Christians there is a threat of following this frame of mind. The church functions as an organization; there are leaders and places of duty. A few people give orders and others need to follow them.

However the leaders are not there to be served but to serve. The church itself doesn't exist to be developed as a power structure; it exists to serve the needs of people. Genuine power isn't that of position however of spiritual influence/persuasion. However, we see such a tiny portion of this sort of power because Christians are hesitant to be slaves and servants.

The great servant slave are the people who are delicate to the necessities of others; they search for opportunities to be empathetic and supportive. They don't consider the consequence to themselves; they are happy to forfeit their very own time and assets if need be to serve another person.

We would all preferably be waited upon at the table over carrying the food ourselves. Be that as it may, in the spiritual domain there must be the people who are happy to be table attendants for Christ, those ready to serve, to tidy up, to do the grimy, unpleasant jobs. Out of such ability comes genuine Christian vitality that can change people.

The Example Of The Saviour
(v. 45)

Jesus lived out what he taught. He was the encapsulation of his own spiritual standards. To get what he was stating here we need just watch him in real life. It is fundamental that we strengthen our psyches (minds) routinely by reading and learning about Jesus in the accounts of the gospels. We are to walk as he walked. To do that, we should be available to the guidance of the Holy Spirit about the servanthood of Jesus Christ.

Jesus characterized his way of life in two different ways: he came to serve and to give. That is our essential example. Thus, we don't find him being attended to in every conceivable way in unassuming conditions, and endure a hand-to-mouth presence. He had no political power base.

He gave himself absolutely to tending to the necessities of others.

At last, it cost him his life. That is the most anybody can give. At the point when we think our service is praiseworthy, we should consider the cross; there is our model, there is our example. Jesus died for our transgressions (sins), as a payment, to set us free. How far would we say we will go for others?

(Get some information about somebody who is great as indicated by Christ's definition. For what reason do they feel this person is great? Request that they write on a piece of paper a few ways by which they can be great this week. For what reason is it difficult to be a servant slave?)

End: Serving and giving are the most elevated desires of life. However these objectives are lost sight on the planet's distraught commotion to excel. Christian homes and churches are the only places where true greatness is taught and exemplified.

Chapter Fifteen

The Way Of Authentic Prayer
(Luke 18:1-14)

THERE ARE SCARCELY ANY people who don't have faith in prayer, yet there additionally are few people who pray consistently and faithfully. Petition for many people is an all in or all out suggestion. They listen to supplications at church and they pray when they get into a difficult situation. Be that as it may, the order of every day prayer is something they are not prepared to accept.

Why seeing this appearing logical inconsistency among profession and practice? Most likely in light of the fact that genuine prayer is diligent work; it requires thought and focus (concentration). Approach somebody to petition God for five minutes and they will think that its difficult to tell what to say to God for that long.

Another explanation is that regularly people believe that petition requires a special kind of sacred or holy language that only a few Christians are gifted at using. They don't comprehend that supplication is a conversation with God. Supplication (prayer) is revealing to God what is on your heart and listening for his answer. It doesn't require practice in using "thee" and "thou," yet it requires transparency and honesty.

People also neglect (fail) to grow great prayer habits because they don't find the various aspects of petition. They know how to request day by day bread and protection, however, they have not learned how to praise God and how to intercede for other people. Finding the wealth in prayer requires investigating all of its many features.

Now and again people don't pray on the grounds that they are not on speaking terms with God. They are living in rebellion, or disobedience; they have not confessed their transgressions (sins). Until they repent and find restoration, they will not converse with God about anything.

In this lesson we perceive how Jesus encouraged persistence and trustworthiness (honesty) in prayer. These are two fundamental elements for a fulfilling prayer life.

We Ought To Pray Persistently
(Luke 18:1-8 KJV)

Jesus didn't make prayer a complicated thing. If we grasp the central point of his teaching here, we will learn how basic prayer is. This parable doesn't tell everything there is to know regarding supplication (prayer), however it teaches that people are rewarded for their persistence in prayer.

The Widow's Petition
(vv. 1-3)

Jesus told this story, while on his last adventure to Jerusalem by way of Samaria and Galilee (A.D. 29, 30). He had quite recently healed the ten lepers and afterward taught about the signs of his second coming.

We are in no uncertainty about the focal application of this story, since it is given in verse 1: "They ought always to pray and not lose heart." This is our clue about persistence in petition.

Having recently heard Jesus portray the fearsome events to come "on the day when the Son of man is revealed" (17:30), his disciples needed this consolation to continue on in prayer. Their persistence in supplication (prayer) will be the sure indication of their faith, which is what Jesus will look for when he come again (v. 8).

Supplication at that point is the remedy for losing heart. Two dispositions (attitudes) toward life are differentiated. All people face upsetting conditions throughout everyday life. The temptation is to surrender (give up), or lose heart, even with preliminaries (trials) and hardships. In any case, genuine true serenity (true peace of mind) comes only by steadfast prayer. "Always" means consistently and in all conditions or circumstances.

To show this principle Jesus told a simple story about a widow who was being victimized and a judge who didn't want to help her. In any case, at long last the vulnerable, helpless widow prevailed.

Jesus portrayed the widow's furthest point. The judge for her situation had no respect for either his duty to God or to men. He was calloused and unscrupulous, so for every single useful reason the widow got no opportunity by any stretch of the imagination.

However there was no other place for the widow to go for help. The judge alone could give her help. Notwithstanding his known notoriety, she "continued coming to him." Apparently she had an admirable motivation, in spite of the fact that we are not determined what it was.

From what we are aware of general social conditions, be that as it may, she was most likely being gouged monetarily by a landowner or bank. Widows had no status by any stretch of the imagination; nobody safeguarded them, so they were helpless before oppressors.

Here in reality was cause for losing heart. The judge represented power and the widow represented shortcoming (weakness). She was overwhelmed by her conditions, however she didn't abandon her lone road of claim. This is the reason she delineates constancy in prayer. She had a particular need and she talked constantly about it.

The disciples could value the widow's trouble. They were confronting the impulse to surrender (give up). They had no political or money related influence to use to get their way. Persecution awaited them. The widow foreshadowed their very own vulnerability, aside from a certain something: prayer. Prayer would enable them to win against overpowering odds.

The Judge's Response
(vv. 4, 5)

The cold-blooded, hard-hearted judge was unaffected by the widow's interests from the start, however then he yielded. Note his explanation behind vindicating her. It was not on the grounds that he stirred to his obligation to God and individuals; it was on the grounds that the widow irritated and destroyed him by her persistent coming. He was essentially constrained into giving in by her determination.

Nobody would have anticipated this result, knowing the conditions. "It's no use," is the manner in which individuals feel when gone up against with clearly sad conditions. Be that as it may, for reasons unknown the widow didn't acknowledge the self-evident. She turned around the conditions, not by control, not by impact, not by pay off, however by faithfulness in carrying her case to the judge.

Jesus Christ's Promise And Question
(vv. 6-8)

To drive home the point of the story to his followers, Jesus expressed a fundamental reality about God and afterward brought up a searching question. In the first place, be that as it may, there was the difference between the unrighteous judge and God.

What had the judge said? "I will vindicate the widow." He did as such disregarding his profane, unrighteous character. How at that point would it be advisable for us to feel about God who is upright? Shall he do any less than the judge? The idea itself is unbelievable, however by and by Jesus forced the disciples and us to consider it.

This question is necessary to uncover our laziness and lack of faith in prayer.

If an unfeeling judge at long last yielded to the widow, shouldn't something be said about a God who cares? Undergirding our confidence in petition is our insight into God himself

We are not to think about him as stubbornly opposing our prayers, but as one who responds "speedily."

Jesus posed two questions: Will not God vindicate his elect? Will he postpone his answer? At that point he responded to the two inquiries directly: "He will vindicate them speedily."

'His elect" are believers, the people who have come to know God through personal faith in

Jesus Christ. Any person who responds to God's invitation to be saved can be a part of his elect. "Whoever believes in him" (John 3:16) is the only condition. "Each one who calls upon the name of the Lord will be saved" (Rom. 10:13).

Believers are imagined as crying to God "day and night." This is a delineation of persistence in supplication. There is no time when prayer isn't needed. On our part, petition can well up in a person's heart whenever, at wherever.

On God's part, his ear is constantly mindful to our cries. God doesn't keep available time; no arrangements are important to converse with him. Day or night the lines to paradise are open, and there are no tolls to be paid.

What is God's response to such supplication from his children? Note the differentiation between "delay long" and "speedily." Delay is a reference to how the indecent judge treated the widow; speedily is a reference to how God responses to believers.

By the by, it appears to us that occasionally our petitions are not addressed rapidly. Christians appeal to God for specific things for a considerable length of time and years, and their solicitations are not allowed. Jesus doesn't answer that issue here.

He doesn't take a look at the particular answers we want, but instead at how God vindicates his own.

Real petition is accepting God's will - his simple treatment of our case - instead of demanding one's narrow minded desires. Supplication (prayer) means all out commitment to God for whatever his answer may mean. His answer probably won't be liberation from a preliminary, yet it may be tolerance to bear the preliminary. That would be our vindication. His answer probably won't be to change our conditions, however to change our attitude toward them. That would be his vindication of us.

To be vindicated doesn't intend to get your own specific way. The thought behind the word vindicate is that of justice. Jesus stated, in actuality, "God will give them justice and protection, and that without delay." We must learn how to trust the case to decide wisely with him, because we can confide in his wisdom and love to give us what is best for us

To pray steadily or persistly means never abandoning who God is, the sovereign of the universe who rules our lives evenhandedly (justly). This idea of God causes us to acknowledge whatever answer he gives.

What is it then that God looks for in our supplication encounters? Persistence and faith. The two go inseparably. In the event that we have no faith, we will not persist. But if we have faith, we shall persist. Prayer is the profoundest exercise of faith. That is the reason Jesus brought up the issue of faith in this context.

In the wake of telling how God responds, Jesus said that the character of God demands faith on our part. God is dependable, He is trustworthy. He isn't to be used like an enchantment wand, but he is to be believed. The enchantment wand's way to deal with prayer recommends that "prayer changes things," however the believing approach to deal with prayer implies that supplication transforms me and my demeanors toward things and conditions. God looks for our faith, our total trust in him. Prayer is the means he has given us to express that faith and trust.

(For what reason don't Christians pray all the more consistently? What are a few obstacles to an effective supplication (prayer) life? What encouragements to prayer do you receive from this parable? What would be advisable for you to do when you have an inclination that your supplications are inadequate? When your requests aren't addressed "quickly"? What guidance in petition would you be able to provide for another Christian?)

We Ought To Pray Honestly
(Luke 18:9-14 KJV)

Two men show up in this story to delineate the need of honesty in prayer. Be that as it may, the one we would hope to have mastered something about prayer - the Pharisee -didn't prevail in his prayer. It was the untouchable, the outsider who knew nothing about the correct structures and words who gained Jesus Christ's approval for his disposition (his attitude) in prayer.

The Pharisee's Dishonesty
(vv. 9-12)

This story was gone for the pompous among the people who followed Jesus (v. 9). They "confided in themselves that they were equitable." These were for the most part the strict religious leaders and the people who prided themselves on their severe devotion to the laws of Israel.

Jesus always conflicted with these people because they saw no compelling reason to repent and accept the gospel. Their trust was in their very own integrity; they lacked the power to deal with Christ and his spiritual demands; they rejected his interests for a difference in heart. Apparently, they kept up the entirety of the necessary strict observances, but Jesus knew their hearts were spoiled (rotten).

The Pharisee in Christ's story represents this pitiful spiritual condition. He demonstrates how it is conceivable to experience the custom of prayer but then overlook what's really important of prayer inside and out. Note the substance of his prayer:

He expressed gratitude toward God for his own integrity and he said thanks to God that he was superior to other people. Thus was his deplorable pride reflected. Jesus didn't close that the Pharisee was lying; obviously the Pharisee was coming clean with God about himself. He was conscientiously strict; he fasted and tithed. He had carried out no incredible violations, or crimes and was devoted to his marriage vows.

How at that point would he say he was untrustworthy? He didn't recount to the entire story about himself. Did he have no transgressions to admit and confess? Clearly he did, yet these didn't ring a bell when he prayed. The Pharisee was so glad for what he had achieved, and he despised sinners so much, that he couldn't force himself to recognize any sins of his own.

His was a deceptive prayer. We give the Pharisee high checks for his strict loyalty. He was the sort of person we might want to have as a neighbor and personal church member.

He speaks to the smug strict people of our day. In any case, his supplication (prayer) got no place in view of his pride in himself and his prevalence over others. He even expressed gratitude toward God that he was superior to the tax collector authority who was praying simultaneously.

As a result, the Pharisee was stating that he merited something from God in light of how good or great he was. Quite a bit of our supplicating depends on that mentality. God by one way or another turns out like Santa Claus, and in the event that you are bad you won't get any presents.

In the event that we accept we can move God that way, obviously we will practice our good or great deeds before him. In any case, the Bible discloses to us that God isn't intrigued by our very own decency, on the grounds that even our best confidence misses the mark regarding his holiness (cf. Rom.3:20, 23).

The Honesty Of The Tax Collector
(v. 13)

Here was a loathed delinquent, a despised sinner setting out to come and supplicate (pray) with the proud Pharisee. Notice how various his methodology was. He came as a modest contrite. He made no misrepresentation of being great or good. He didn't attempt to intrigue God with his accomplishments. The tax collector basically came clean about himself.

He doesn't have anything great to present? Obviously he did; he was not absolutely terrible. There were some good characteristics about him, but when he supplicated (prayed) he was concerned about only a single thing: his acknowledgment by a holy, honest, righteous God.

The tax collector realized the tremendous bay between God's holiness and his transgression (sin). He knew there was no expectation (hope) for himself, aside from God's leniency (mercy). In this way, he confessed his transgression and requested God's mercy. He realized the judgment was genuine, but supplication to God could be the means for forgiveness and pardoning.

His genuineness in supplication comprised basically in his coming clean with God about himself. That is difficult to do, but it is essential since misleading God only defers the inescapable judgment, and what's more you can't conceal anything from God at any rate.

Authentic supplication develops out of this sort of transparency. We have no case on God; we don't have anything to bring to procure any favors from him. That is an inappropriate methodology; that is the human-focused methodology. We like to intrigue people with our accomplishments, but God isn't dazzled on the grounds that our transgressions (sins) are so shocking to him. His righteousness is outraged by our autonomy, pride, and waywardness.

How reviving and purifying it is then to converse with God like the tax collector did. That is the best way to find help and significant serenity. We should "come out with the simple truth of the matter" with God. There is no reason for gloating and no reason for holding back. God's Holy Spirit motivates us to be straightforward, honest in prayer.

Jesus Christ's Evaluation
(v. 14)

Which man was "justified" by his supplication involvement with the temple? If we somehow managed to take a look at the two men as per their ethical records, we would need to state that the Pharisee was justified. In any case, Jesus didn't take a look at them that way. He took a look at their inward frames of mind toward God, as reflected by their prayers.

The affected Pharisee stayed under judgment, since he commended himself before God. The repentant tax collector was forgiven and justified by God because he lowered (humbled) himself before God. This was a finished inversion of the human desire in this circumstance. Be that as it may, the tax collector got a handle on the significant standard of humiliation and confession before a holy and righteous God.

With regards to our supplication encounters, we should pursue a similar methodology. Our only claim on God is his benevolence (mercy); there is no reason for boasting about our legitimacy. In any case, what right do we have to request mercy?

Is it true that we are not all under condemnation and judgment?

Obviously, we are, yet Jesus died for our transgressions (sins) and rose once more, taking our judgment upon himself. The author of Hebrews clarified it thusly: "Along these lines, brethren, since we have confidence to enter the sanctuary by the blood of Jesus, by the new and living way...let us draw near with a true heart in full assurance of faith" (10:19, 20, 22). This is all the encouragement we have to supplicate. Our sins need not shield us from chatting with a blessed, righteous, holy God. We may intensely draw near as the tax collector did, requesting benevolence (mercy) based on Jesus Christ's work for us.

(For what reason is it difficult to be straightforward with Gods? For what reason do we want to dazzle God with our acts of kindness? How great would you must be before God could hear and answer your supplications? What part does confession play in supplication? How regularly would it be advisable for you to confess your transgressions? How might one make preparations for false quietude? What should a person experience from Jesus Christ to be totally free and open in his supplications before God? Why?)

End: God has made every provision for us to converse with him. We lose our spiritual vitality when we disregard day by day discussion with him. Confession, praise, and prayer are needed, both to our benefit and for God's glory. God made us for personal fellowship. We who have been redeemed ought disappointment him.

Chapter Sixteen

The Way Of Forgiving Love
(Luke 15:17-32 KJV)

THE WORLD IS LOADED with prodigals. Who of us sooner or later has not gone off to some far away place from our heavenly Father's will? However a strain of vain glory continues. We might want to feel that we are not as awful as the extravagant child in the story Jesus told.

The facts confirm that not every person encounters a similar debasement of transgression (sin), however any deviation from God's righteousness is sufficient to censure us. Regardless of whether our good deeds exceed our terrible ones, we are evenhandedly blameworthy by God.

Nobody can rightly point their finger at the more clear prodigals among us. We as a whole know people - our children maybe - who have rejected God's truth, his standards, and his good news of salvation. Yet, we are not to be taken up with accusations and tattle about the people who have strayed.

Maybe the narrative of the extravagant child (prodigal son) time and again has filled in as a take off platform for tirades against the follies of youth. The Christian feels hurt when he sees anybody unearth sin, and there is a place for correction and reproof. Yet in his story Jesus made significantly more of how the father got back his erring son than he did of the son's transgression (sin).

Our general public (society) today puts great weight on people to kick over moral and spiritual restraints. Scriptural norms are rejected as outmoded. They are replaced by popular vote, in a manner of speaking, where the dominant part chooses (the majority). If enough people accomplish something, it must be OK. Legislators talk about "decriminalizing" certain conduct.

Consequently, when people succumb to this thinking they end up caught as the prodigal son seemed to be. Step by step instructions to contact them with love, acceptance, and forgiveness becomes a significant and major concern of Christians. This lesson should help us with seeing the concern in a fresh light.

The Repentant Son
(Luke 15:17-24 KJV)

Jesus told to the narratives recorded in Luke 15 toward the start of his ministry in Peraea close to the end of A.D. 29. The quick setting was the objection (complaint) of the scribes and Pharisees that Jesus was excessively well disposed with miscreants (too friendly with sinners) (vv. 1, 2).

To clarify why he offered himself to these social outsiders, Jesus taught three parables regarding the lost sheep, a lost coin, and a lost son. Every story ended with a note of rejoicing in light of the fact that the lost had been found. So Jesus Christ's mission then and now is to find people who know they are lost in sin.

The Prodigal Son's Change Of Mind
(vv. 17-19)

The lesson content starts at an urgent defining moment in the life of the reckless. He was the younger of two children in his family and had demanded his share of his father's estate. In any case, "he wasted his property in free (loose, wild) living" (v. 13). That is the manner by which he came to be known as the prodigal son, despite the fact that Jesus didn't use that word to portray him.

Subsequently, he wound up in a sad circumstance: no cash, no companions, no nourishment. In that condition "he started thinking clearly." As we would say, he woke up to the realities; he altered his perspective (changed his mind) on what was attractive and desirable throughout everyday life and came to see the appalling slip-up and tragic mistake he had made.

The young man began figuring he could find fulfillment in having heaps of cash to purchase companions and a good time. Somehow, many people are propelled by similar considerations today. That is their solitary reason throughout everyday life, to make enough cash to get the things they think will fulfill them or make them happy.

Reality with regards to significance and reason in life lies somewhere else, but since we are born sinners we continue going our own specific way. We don't need God to teach us. We don't to be trimmed in by his principles. In this way, eventually - if we are truly to discover what life is about - we need to alter our perspectives. We need to change our pondering both our points throughout everyday life and about God's will.

The reckless saw his actual condition - "I perish with hunger" - and contrasted it and what was accessible at home: "bread enough to spare." He didn't disregard his needs; he didn't claim to have a great time when he wasn't. He didn't trust that some way or another things would show signs of improvement. Until a person remembers, "I perish," he won't be inspired to make a fundamental spiritual change.

Be that as it may, what could the intemperate do? He had requested his entitlement to be autonomous. Would he be able to return as a son? The fascination of home was strong because he was so eager, yet might he be able to really concede that he had committed a mistake? That is a hard activity, however he chose to do it.

He would recognize his transgressions against God and against his father. He would concede that his wrongdoing (sin) excluded him from being his father's son. He would request to be treated as a hired servant. Here is an image of complete repentance. To abandon one's transgression back to God requires a simple acknowledgment.

We don't have anything qualified to bring to God; just our confession that we have trespassed against him. We reserve no option to be viewed as his child. Until we confess our articulate misery and weakness, we can't establish a saving relationship with our heavenly Father.

His Forgiveness
(v. 20)

What do you think the young man expected to get when he returned home? A rebuke? A chastening? An "I told you so" address? Most likely, however he chose to return home in any case and "recognize the cold hard reality."

By his difference at the top of the priority list he was prepared for whatever results may come. He realized he merited some reprimand and discipline for his wrongdoings (sins).

In any case, he likewise was persuaded that his father was a reasonable, simple man. There must be something about their relationship in the past that would lead him to put himself helpless before his father. Throughout the years he had come to trust and respect his father, despite the fact that he had gone his own particular way.

By the by, his father's respond catches us unsuspecting. We are not prepared for this kind gathering. The father essentially welcomed him; he embraced and kissed his errant child. His sympathy and warmth were profusely showing.

The father could have bolted him out; he could have constrained him to languish longer over his transgressions. In any case, he took him in without a talk, without an expression of analysis. His affection for his child was extraordinary to the point that he forgave him.

Here we see the genuine idea of forgiveness. It is unconstrained and ungrudging; it requests nothing in return. Forgiving isn't blow for blow; it is essentially eradicating the past offenses. Forgiveness means tolerating the guilty party as he may be, not holding a club of requital over his head.

God acknowledges us thusly in Christ. He grasps and kisses each humble heathen. His easy-going adoration is unreservedly given; there is nothing we can do to acquire it.

As we turn toward him in repentance and faith, he reaches out assure us that we are accepted. The Holy Spirit confirms in our hearts that God has forgiven us. We can accept God's forgiveness because Jesus Christ took capital punishment (death penalty) we merited for our sins.

The father in this story speaks to how "God forgives us and how we are to forgive others. In any case, often Christians think that its difficult to be so open and accepting, even with their own youngsters. It is difficult to let free the dynamic power of love. We would prefer to be judges and pundits than forgivers.

To forgive doesn't mean taking a light perspective on transgression (sin), just as though sin doesn't make a difference. It is the inverse. Because sin is so shockingly grievous, forgiveness is so costly.

In the event that sin were no offense, for what reason would it be advisable for us to forgive? God's forgiving costs him his Son on Calvary's cross. If we are to forgive one who has annoyed us, it will cost us our pride and our entitlement to correct retaliation. Sin hurts, so it hurts to forgive.

His Confession
(v. 21)

It is one thing to conjecture about making an confession; it is another to complete one's expectations. Numerous people plan eventually to get their lives fixed with God, yet when the open door returns they back off. Not so with the reckless. Would it be advisable for him to proceed with his confession, seeing that his father had invited him back so lavishly? Why not skip it, since he makes certain of his father's adoration? If these musings struck the young man, they didn't prevent him from making his confession.

He recognized bad behavior(wrongdoings) against God and his father, and he conceded that he had precluded himself from sonship in the family.

The young man's actual spiritual change needed to become exposed. If repentance is real, it will be communicated. It will prompt an adjustment seeing someone. Sin makes fellowship impossible on both the divine and human levels.

Repentance and confession dispel any confusion air on the guilty party (offender); forgiveness eliminates any confusion air on the person who has been offended. That is the reason they resemble different sides of a coin. Both must happen if restoration and fellowship are to be established.

His Celebration
(vv. 22-24)

The reckless, prodigal said he did not merit being called his father's son, however the father had different plans. He would not accept his son's proposition, despite the fact that he may have done so as a result of his son's takeoff and waywardness. Rather, he organized an extraordinary festival (banquet).

His son showed up home down and out and hungry, so the father requested new garments for him and nourishment to eat. They would have a meal for him. The son would never again yearn for corn grain in the hog pens; he would feast on his father's best nourishment - so complete was his forgiveness and restoration.

Here is a lovely picture of how the father exhibited his forgiveness and acceptance. He masterminded the best for his son. So God our Father accomplishes for us when he forgives us; he not only starts all over again (wipe the slate clean), he sustains us on the eternal wealth of Jesus Christ.

He blesses us with every single spiritual blessing; he makes us joint heirs with Christ; he gives us new garments of exemplary nature; to put it plainly, God commends our arrival by making us new people. Rather than being wayward and rebellious, we become his obedience children; we are fully adopted into his family.

The festival (banquet) was advocated on the grounds that "my son was dead, and is alive again; he was lost, and is found." Apparently the father never expected to see his son again. The way that he was home again was adequate reason to celebrate. In any case, the father's heart without a doubt was heartened in light of the fact that his son had confessed his transgression (sin).

He didn't return dreary, defiant and rebellious; he returned changed in attitude. The prodigal was a son in more than name only; he was completely forgiven and restored.

(How are we as a whole like the prodigal son? Do you think he expected to be forgiven? Why or why not? For what reason is it difficult to request forgiveness from God? From other people? For what reason is it difficult to allow forgiveness? In what ways can we "Make joyful" when lost sinners are found? How does your church show the repentant that they are genuinely forgiven and received in full fellowship? For what reason do we regularly think that its difficult to forgive those whom God has forgiven?)

The Jealous Son
(Luke 15:25-32 KJV)

The third primary character in the prable presently shows up, the desirous senior son (older son). He couldn't comprehend and accept his father's easy-going frame of mind toward his younger brother. The Lord Jesus incorporated his response in the story with the goal that we may keep away from the catch of an envious, unforgiving spirit.

His Anger
(vv. 25-28a)

The elder son was out working in the fields when the festival began, but he before long discovered what was happening. He was sat originally confused by what he heard, so he got some information about it. The hireling gave a brief yet sufficient report; the festival was on the grounds that the lost younger son had come back home and his father had received him.

Huge news! Be that as it may, the elder brother bristled at the report. Rather than being happy that his blundering younger brother had returned, he was furious and declined to being happy that his failing brother had returned. Along these lines, he will not participate in the gathering.

How unreasonable human instinct is. Regularly people celebrate when others turn out badly. "Teaches you a lesson," they state. What's more, when the person who has strayed is reestablished, regularly there is doubt, uncertainty, and analysis.

Now and then the people who return are avoided as much as possible. We feel they can't be completely trusted in view of their past errors. These frames of mind are an impression of an unforgiving heart.

His Complaint
(vv. 28b-30)

The father had no chance to ask his more youthful son to return home, yet now he should go out to his elder son and approach him to come in for the festival. How patient he was with them two in their blunders.

With the equivalent paternal empathy with which he grasped the extravagant, the father begged his furious child to be a part of the family.

Be that as it may, he was rebuked. His elder son answered luxuriously. He was immaculate and his father was to blame. He protested at the rich consideration being used on a ne'er-progress admirably. He blamed his father for neglecting to treat him in a similar free and upbeat way.

He rushed to blame his more youthful brother for squandering his father's cash on whores. He couldn't force himself to concede that the reckless was his very own brother; he called him "this son of yours." How terrible he was of his father's love, forgiveness, and rejoicing.

The eldeer son could only observe his own decency (good) rather than his brother's disappointments. To him it was totally out of line that he ought to never have been given a "kid" rather than "the fatted calf" his brother had gotten.

This shows he overlooked what's really important of the festival. It was anything but a gathering for the amusement and delight of the prodigal and his companions; it was an expression of the joy the father felt at the recovery of his son.

As it were, the elder son was "lost" despite the fact that he never ventured out from home. His basic, unforgiving spirit cast him past the range of his father's love. Not so his father was heartless (as we will see), however the elder son didn't appreciate what he was receiving right along.

He needed requital for his more youthful brother, not a cheerful festival. The disclosure of the lost and the resurrection of the dead were events for joy, yet the elder son missed the joy as a result of his bitter heart.

His Rebuke
(vv. 31, 32)

The father would not blow up at his child's analysis. He just helped him to remember the diverse status of his children and of his total arrangement for him: "all that is mine is yours." How had the elder son missed these steadfast tokens of his father's love? He had gotten everything. How could be resent his sibling a gathering? His heart was so off key that his explanation was mutilated.

So the father clarifies why he was celebrating. It was fitting a result of the spiritual change that had happened; the lost had been found; the dead, made alive. There was no exceptional motivation to set the family unit rejoicing over the elder son, since he had served his father faithfully.

In any case, here was something unique. How could a father disregard something like a lost son's return and not show his forgiveness, his wonder, his enjoyment?

The spiritual standard is clear: The further a person strays from God, the more abundance he feels at his return. This doesn't mean we ought to charm ourselves in wrongdoing only to have a wonderful return, but it means we ought not be resenting when the prodigals do return.

Preferably, we should serve God as dependably as the elder son served his father. In the event that we acknowledge his nonstop goodness as an impression of his adoration, at that point we will not be disenchanted when a reckless atones and encounters an great bit of God's affection. We will likely be as forgiving and as upbeat as the intemperate's father seemed to be.

Did the elder son in the long run join the gathering and acknowledge his sibling back as a person from the family? Jesus purposely excluded that detail. The elder son speaks to the Pharisees and the story was an intrigue to them to get the outsiders. Jesus was hanging tight for their choice.

(How would you think the tax collectors and sinners felt when they heard this story? The scribes and Pharisees? For what reason do you think the elder son didn't share his father's eagerness and satisfaction at he reckless' (prodigal's) return? For what reason do Christians once in a while miss the celebrating over what God is doing among sinners? Is it feasible for a Christian to loathe not having encountered sin the way a portion of his brothers in Christ did before they became Christians?)

The characteristics of forgiving affection are difficult to characterize, however we are intrigued when we see them in others. The father in this story showed those characteristics. He is the example of our easy-going affection. We are encompassed by lost prodigals who are spiritually dead. Maybe what they need, if they are to be found, is to see forgiveness in the lives of Christians. Such forgiving streams from veritable, unselfish love.

Chapter Seventeen

The Way Of Responsible Stewardship
(Luke 16:10-15; Mark 12:41-44 KJV)

STEWARDSHIP IN SOME CHURCHES delivers a negative response. It may be related with a yearly raising support crusade and with messages about giving more money to meet the congregation's spending plan (budget). Then again, realizing how touchy a few people are about their cash, a few pastors have been known to keep away from the subject through and through.

In some cases individuals outside the congregation get the idea that churches are intrigued basically in money. They are asked to belittle church bazaars and other raising support occasions which may be done for the sake of religion. Subsequently, to certain individuals, attempting to blend cash and religion resembles attempting to blend oil and water.

In any case, the Lord Jesus Christ indicated no hesitance in discussing money. He realized that it was so essential to people. The scribes and

Pharisees got some information about making good on regulatory obligations to Caesar. Money was a hot issue at that time and now.

The principle concern of the Christian is to relate the utilization of his cash to his obedience to Jesus Christ. In the lives of numerous believers their wallets are the last thing to be moved by Christ's lordship. The Christians can't pardon himself from mindful stewardship as a result of supposed maltreatment and contortions in church money raising practices.

A few strategies for raising the financial backing are frightful and not according to biblical standards. However the Christian must endeavor to show that giving is a spiritual blessing, not a pounding burden to he laid on people during special campaigns.

In this lesson we shall find how Jesus called for obedience to God in the use of money. He also cited a poor widow for instance of one who had captured the true spirit of sacrifice for the kingdom of God.

Faithful In Stewardship
(Luke 16:10-15 KJV)

The general pubic (society) of Jesus Christ's time was pointedly isolated between those who are well off and the poor. There was no well-to-do working class as we probably am aware of it today. Truth be told, the normal American would have been viewed as wealthy back then. We live in a novel time ever. At no other time in any one age in one country have such a large number of people had so much to such an extent.

Along these lines, as according to the principles of Jesus, our responsibility is the more noteworthy. In these verses he shows that the manner in which we use our money is an indicator of our spiritual health. The catchphrase (keyword) here is "faithfulness to God" in light of all he has endowed to us.

The Basic Principle
(v. 10)

Jesus had been talking about a dishonest manager who had made an wise deal for himself (vv. 1-9). Now he moves emphasis to show how everyone has a responsibility regarding the wise use of money. He knew that it was significant for his disciples to comprehend various general principles of stewardship.

The use of these principles to one's Christian life is a critical step to spiritual maturity. As we shall see, one's use of money is like a spiritual barometer.

There are two differentiations here: "faithfulness" and dishonesty," and little and much. The truth of the matter is the same in either case. The manner in which a person goes about (acts as) as a steward of a little, regardless of whether honestly or dishonestly, shows how that person will act as a steward of much. Faithfulness depends not on the amount entrusted, but on the sense of responsibility.

This principle is ignored or neglected by some, who feel that it doesn't make a difference on the that you waste a minimal expenditure, or take a minimal expenditure, or cheat a tad. Be that as it may, Jesus built up the need of the "little." This is on the grounds that the "little" is a test of our faithfulness. In the event that we bomb that test, we will likewise bomb the bigger one.

So the steward of God has a constant augmentation of obligation. God knows how we utilize the little endowments he gives. If we neglect to look for his will in the use of limited quantities, we likewise will bomb when we come into more money.

Selfishness (or Childishness) is built up right off the bat in life when we don't have a lot. Providing for God's work in like manner must turn into a habit from the early years, in any event, when we can't bear the cost of it.

In this manner, it is significant for parents to discuss family spending plans with their children. Children should realize that God's will is the main thought in how mother and father use their salary. Children can be encouraged that their stipends and income are not "theirs" however the Lord's.

This is the Christian use of faithfulness "in a very little." If we don't start to do this at an early age, dependability "in much" will be hard to accomplish later on throughout everyday life.

Faithfulness Tested
(vv. 11, 12)

Jesus posed two inquiries to show how faithfulness is tested. These inquiries really are admonitions (warnings), because they are intended to show the results of unfaithfulness. Twice Jesus says, "if you have not been faithful..." What did he mean by that?

His thought returns to the steward who squandered his master's merchandise (goods) (v. 1). The concept of faithfulness here is identified with money, or to anything that has been given us as a trust. A steward is one whom the estate has been endowed (entrusted). Every person is a steward of something; the amount isn't significant.

God is the proprietor (owner) of the universe; he gives us things to use in this life. These things don't generally turn into our own; God doesn't move privileges of possession. The money we have, for instance, is truly God's, but he allows us its use. How are we to use it. Faithfully.

The faithful steward uses his money according to the master's plans, not according to his own. The faithful steward is a careful manager; he wouldn't like to squander (waste) any of his master's assets.

To be unfaithful in this setting is to be childish, pointless, inhumane, and unreliable. It is to go about as though the money is yours, to do with however you see fit, to think nothing about a future bookkeeping of it before God.

As far as one's family spending plan (the budget), the faithful Christian steward will haul out what he trusts God needs him to provide for his work first. He will choose what his necessities and commitments, and what his fixed costs are.

He will put an utmost on what he spends over that, declining to purchase something since he can manage the cost of it (afford it). He will willfully acknowledge a lower expectation for everyday comforts; he will settle on his money related choices with much petition.

Now note Christ's first warning. If a person is a poor steward of money, he won't be entrusted with true, that is, spiritual riches. The utilization of our money is a test of our spiritual vitality. A person may see himself as a committed Christian, yet in the event that he is thrifty (tight-fisted) with his money, he is unspiritual.

Money becomes a snare to our spiritual progress; it is a temptation to rich and poor alike. That is the reason Jesus consistently warned the rich of their spiritual peril. He advised his disciples not to collect riches, but to give it away.

When we search for reasons why churches and individual Christians are not growing in faith and obedience, we can without much of a stretch find one here. Liberal, unselfish Christians make strong churches, churches that are rich in spending plans (budgets) as well as in evangelism, missions, and social concern.

Stewardship is a drudgery if it means exacting money from unfaithful stewards, but it is a joy when it is the unconstrained overflowing of assets from faithful stewards.

The second warning (v. 12) expresses that if a man can't practice appropriate care over a trust given to him, for which he can be brought to account, he won't be given wealth of his own to use however he sees fit.

Once more, this is a sound principle of human management. Nobody would choose a manager of his bequest who has misused his very own cash. However, what is the spiritual application here?

"That which is another's" would appear to allude to all that we have as a trust from God. "That which is your own" would point to our everlasting reward. This pursues a similar contrast in v. 11 between money ("unrighteous mammon") and genuine wealth (true riches).

Once more, we see that one's use of money is a proving ground of his commitment to God and his will. In this life the sum total of what we have is given to us on trust.

If according to God's bookkeeping we are judged faithful, he will give us something as our own property. Now we are on post trial supervision (probation), in a manner of speaking; in the life to come the faithful stewards will have secure, rightful possession and pleasure in all God graciously gives them.

The Faithful Steward's Basic Commitment (v. 13)

People don't prefer to be constrained into either-or circumstances, choices and decisions. They would lean toward both-and, that is, to have their cake and eat it, as well. They might want to have God around, tip him a smidgen on Sunday, and afterward continue utilizing every one of his benefits for their very own selfish ends.

Be that as it may, Jesus said that this disposition can never be translated as faithfulness to God. Such a mentality is, that of an unfaithful steward.

The explanation behind his statement is that God requires absolute loyalty and obedience from his stewards. God doesn't need stewards who cheat him, who attempt to say, "Truly, Lord," and yes to self simultaneously. To be a faithful steward is a win big or bust proposition (an all-or-nothing) with God.

This isn't on the grounds that God is attempting to be mean and stingy with his servants. Jesus clarified that in the order of life no one can be completely responsible to two supervisors. Orders will conflict, loyalties will be separated, so the outcome will be love and hatred.

To serve in this setting intends to be totally at the command of. The symbolism is that of slavery in the ancient world, which didn't allow a division of work or devotion. Masters made elite claims. In any case, in our lives rival bosses compete for our faithfulness and service. For this situation, the opponents (rivals) are God and mammon, or money.

Jesus proclaimed that to be in the service of God one must desert the service of money. God and money are in firm uncompromising vibe (hostility) toward one another ("hate... love...devoted to...despise"). This reveals how looking through this principle is when applied to stewardship. There is no center ground.

Hardly any individuals would concede that they "serve mammon," yet when you take a look at the time and exertion they put into earning more money, you find that money is their god. Not money itself, maybe, but all that money represents to them.

Second occupations, investment plans, lotteries, and over- time all cause significant damage in marriage and family breakdown. They all are a part of serving mammon. What is your god? It is whatever you give your time, strength, and enthusiasm and interest to.

The Pharisees Rebuked
(vv. 14, 15)

Here we get familiar with an intriguing reality about the Pharisees, the individuals who set the standards of piety. They "were admirers (lovers) of money." Jesus had blamed them for hypocrisy, and now he relates their phoniness to their frame of mind (their attitude) to money.

They laughed at the solid demands Jesus made about money. His statement, "You can't serve God and mammon," stirred their fury since they were attempting to join the quest for riches with their severe strict religious observances. To them, riches (wealth) was verification that you were righteous. To be rich and righteous was to have the best of the both worlds.

In any case, they couldn't deny Jesus Christ's rationale, so they scorned him and scoffed at him. This was evidence that his reality had struck a sore spot.

Jesus the exposed their twofold (double) standard. The Pharisees could look good before men, however God knew their hearts. They may have given the appearance of godliness, but in truth the secret of their hearts made them a cursed thing to God.

"What is exalted among men" alludes to their affection for pomp, wealth, and prestige. People of wealth appreciate the status it gives them according to other people. Be that as it may, here is a warning that what people love in such manner is the thing that God despises. The faithful steward will make guard against setting his desires on an inappropriate (wrong) things. Money itself isn't evil, however it applies such a solid fascination upon us that we can before long be lured away from our first love for Jesus Christ.

(Ask that friends determine what the word stewardship passes on to them. Ask that they list descriptors that would depict an unfaithful steward. A faithful steward. What frame of mind or what attitude would be advisable for one to have toward himself to acknowledge the job of a steward? What else is involved with stewardship beside money? What burdens exist in the public eye today that push you to entertain yourself instead of deny yourself? In what way would Christians be able to oppose the strain to procure more to spend more? What necessities have you purchased that used to be extravagances? Where would you be able to draw the line?)

Sacrifice In Stewardship
(Mark 12:41-44 KJV)

The Old Testament incorporates explicit standards for giving. Taken together, all the necessary offering added up to in excess of 30% for the faithful Israelite. The New Testament sets out no particular figure or rate. As noted above, Jesus taught faithfulness and responsibility in the use of everything, on the grounds that we have been given everything by God. Such faithfulness grows out putting yourself absolutely at the disposal of the Lord.

Jesus also demonstrated that faithfulness demands penance (sacrifice), giving that hurts. He did this by differentiating the giving of the rich people with that of a poor widow. Here was an object lesson we can't miss. When we grasp the widow's spirit we will not be concerned about living up to a bare minimum tithe for the Lord.

The Giving Of The Rich And Poor
(vv. 41, 42)

The scene is "the treasury," not a special building but rather part of the sanctuary in Jerusalem. Along the corridor which encompassed the Court of the Women there were thirteen chests with trumpet-molded openings accommodated for the offerings of the worshipers. Jesus sat at some vantage point in full perspective on this part of the temple.

He saw the rich people placing in "enormous sums" and he saw a poor widow placing in two coins, so little in esteem that together they approached only one Roman penny. Among these rich people without a doubt were the devout scribes and Pharisees. The widow by complexity was no one important in the public arena (No one in society).

Jesus Christ's Evaluation Of Their Giving (vv. 43, 44)

Had we been watching the scene, particularly in the event that we had been answerable for meeting the temple spending plan, we would have been pleased with the enormous aggregates, however not dazzled with the two coppers. We would have figured our assessment carefully by the sum given. So today we are dazzled by enormous benefactors, however not by the individuals who can't give much without a doubt.

Jesus didn't assess (evaluate) the givers by the sum they gave. Indeed, he said the widow really gave more than all the rich individuals. That wasn't valid as far as dollars and pennies, obviously. How at that point could Jesus say that the "widow has placed in additional"?

She gave more since she "put in all that she had, her entire living," while the rich gave out of wealth." What rule does Jesus Christ teach here about stewardship? It's not the amount you give that matters, but the level of sacrifice included. Or then again, to put it another way, it's not the amount you give away, yet the amount you have left over that matters.

This is the reason you can't say a Christian must give a specific sum (10%), for instance. That may be a lot for a few, and insufficient for other people. The widow represents express, total sacrifice. That is Christ's standard. She gave "her whole living," which means she didn't have anything left, not in any event, for necessities like nourishment (food).

Along these lines, when Jesus takes a look at our giving he takes a look at our intentions (motives). This is the thing that offers an incentive to our stewardship, not the dollar sum. The genuine estimation of each blessing is relative, not total, since it relies upon how profoundly into one's belongings the supplier has chosen to dig. Hence, the person who can't give huge sums, but who gives sacrifically, is extremely the faithful steward.

Proportionate giving is the thing that God expects of his stewards (cf. II Cor. 8:12). The

Christians in the houses of worship (churches) of Macedonia exhibited this spirit in the early church (II Cor. 8:1-5). Jesus Christ's assessment of a praiseworthy offering isn't our plenitude, however our inadequacy; not what will never be missed, but what costs us some true sacrifice.

As Christians, we are under Jesus Christ's investigation of our giving. Despite everything he sits somewhere near the treasury, so to speak, and watches what we put in when the plate is passed.

At that time our commitment and sacrifice are tried and uncovered. What we give away will reveal the amount we love and trust him.

Jesus Christ's consistent accentuation was give, give, give. He cautioned against the perils of wanting things, in light of the fact that the genuine importance of life isn't to be found in assets. Faithful stewardship will help us with finding the genuine (true) importance of life.

(Have your companions to assess their very own offering as indicated by all accounts. Have them compose their reaction on note paper. How many different needs do you think about that could be met by giving? In what zones would you be able to be a faithful steward notwithstanding your congregation budgeting plan? By what method can a Christian assess the numerous interests that come to him for money?)

Determination: A steward perceives that everything is given to him as a trust from God. He also realizes that caring belongings for the good of their own makes it difficult to love God and fellow men. In this manner, he searches for chances to show sacrificial love and concern by keeping away from unnecessary acquisitions and by giving liberally and happily.

Chapter Eighteen

Jesus Offers Himself
(Mark 11:7-10; 14:32-36; 15:33-39)

THE FUNDAMENTAL COMPONENTS OF Holy Week are: Triumph, Agony, and Crucifixion. Natural? Truly, as far as our knowing the authentic certainties. Be that as it may, Holy Week every year allows us to make the realities personal. It isn't only that Jesus suffered and died, but that he suffered and died for me.

The world will make a cursory effort during the seven day stretch of remembering Jesus Christ's triumphal entry and his enthusiasm on Calvary's cross. For some, this will be the degree of their Christian duty. They will assume that they are Christians since they participate in the unique observances of the week.

The people who take an interest in this caring nominal Christianity are not prone to pray as Jesus did, "Father, not what I will, but what thou wilt." That is the most difficult commitment of all - the commitment of one's own will to God.

We find that its hard in regular daily life to take orders from another person. Youngsters don't care to bow to their parents, nor parents to their supervisors, and none of us like to bow before all-powerful God. This is on the grounds that the substance of transgression (sin) lies in our needing to do however we see fit. Selfishness and freedom cause us to demand having our own particular way, regardless of whether in human relations or in our relations with God.

Holy Week drives us to consider the one in particular who was never sinful, never disobedient, never insistence on his own way. However on account of our transgressions, Jesus Christ had to acknowledge the cup of torturous killing (crucifixion). It was a costly matter; it was difficult.

We are pardoned and forgiven of transgression (sin) today simply because Jesus bowed to his Father's will. Seeing him in triumph, agony, and torturous killing (crucifixion) during the Holy Week should make us ask whether we are totally submitted to God's will. Or on the other hand is this week the time we leave God a tip, as it were, for his favors?

Jesus Christ's Triumphal Entry
(Mark 11:7-10 NIV)

The main scene of Holy Week happens out and about from Bethany to Jerusalem. It is a striking scene of triumph and praise; it is a parade to pay tribute to the Lord Jesus Christ; he is the focal figure; everything focuses to him. There is no challenge for prizes in this procession. The challenge here is between the cases of Christ and the cases of the nation's strict religious leaders, who said he was a phony, a cheat, and a blasphemer.

His Procession
(vv. 7, 8)

The Lord Jesus rode into Jerusalem on an unbroken colt (11:2). He had neither seat nor cover, so he sat on the garments of his companions. Roused by the presence of one who professed to be God's Son and Israel's Messiah, people removed their external pieces of clothing and tossed them on the ground before the yearling. Others immediately cut a few branches from close by trees and made a floor covering out of them.

Jesus knew where his mount was to be found, however, other than this was an alternative parade.

He had no advance men to set up (prepare) the way, to prepare the crowds, to deliver pennants and banners and confetti.

However, this basic immediacy of the event was catching. As opposed to the fake and the fabricated, this was an outpouring of the hopes and desires that griped numerous individuals. Jesus might not have been the choice of the establishment to run the nation, however he was the decision of the average folks who responded to him happily.

The refined or sophisticated among them more likely than not wondered, be that as it may, at the nonappearance of glory and grandeur. How could a man professed to be God's anointed come to the capital in such a modest, lowly fashion as this? Without a doubt this probably appeared to be a frail endeavor at gaining power.

As we look back, we see that the style of Jesus Christ's entrance fit the character of his kingship. Jesus Christ was in reality no military hero going ahead a war horse, nor was he the political revolutionary the oppressed, subjected Jews expected would deliver them from their Roman overlords.

However he merited all the respect, honor and majesty these basic people could give him, the people who knew little what was coming. Jesus was not going to oust Rome, but a far more worse burden of bondage - the power of sin.

His Acclamation
(vv. 9, 10)

Some people wanted to be at the head of the procession and some wanted to raise the back (bring up the rear). We have no clue what number of people were there, but it more likely than not been an extensive number since Jesus had excited colossal enthusiasm by his miracles and his lessons.

The group cried in praise and in hope, "Hosanna!" which signifies, "Save Now." The equivalent is recorded in Psalm 118:25, where it is comprehended to allude to the Messiah. The people communicated a burst of esteem far more extensive and more profound than at any other time heard before.

They articulated a blessing on Jesus, first because they remembered he was coming "for the sake of the Lord," and second since they found in him the restoration of David's kingdom. This was the loftiest style where Jesus could be acclaimed as the promised deliverer.

This was a shout of faith as well as hope. The God-fearing people were tuned to the incredible predictions (prophecies) of the Old Testament. They connected Messiah with the glory of king David. They knew he was of David's line. Jesus Christ's power was shown over and over. He completely merited and deserved the praise and the commendations they gave him.

We know how rapidly the tide betrayed Jesus, however that ought not make us lose the noteworthiness of this event. Only as we consider the to be Jesus as Christ the Lord and King can we completely acknowledge what occurred on Good Friday.

Jesus came to the people as God's Son and David's successor. The approval (acclamation) was well-established. Today we praise him since he lives as King, having vanquished sin and death. As we think about this scene, we need to ask ourselves, What acclaim (praise), glory, and blessing do we bring to Jesus? What garments of our own do we spread before him to demonstrate our regard to him as our King?

(Request that your companions give their impressions of this scene. Had you been there, what might have dazzled you about Jesus? About the people? What tensions would you have felt? What hopes? What motivates people today to be open and unrestrained in their praise of Jesus? What hinders them from giving praise?)

Jesus Christ's Testing In The Garden (Mark 14:32-36 NIV)

This scene brings us into the most profound desolation (agony) in the life of Jesus Christ. He has come to zero time in God's plan. From the beginning he recognized what his mission was. He told the disciples repeatedly that he would be executed; now the time has arrived.

What he had thought about so smoothly, so calmly now turns into a snapshot of severe anguish. This is suffering of the most shocking kind. We all, as we consider telling God we want his will to be done in our lives, come to the heart of the matter where we say, "Truly, God, but not that." And God says, "Yes, that." For Jesus, it was preliminary (trial), mocking, scourging, and torturous killing via crucifixion. God has enabled us to see how he faced it.

His Great Distress
(vv. 32-34)

This scene happens in Gethsemane, a garden nursery at the foot of the Mount of Olives close to Jerusalem. (Gethsemane signifies "olive press.") Jesus and his disciples had regularly gone there (John 18:2). Presently, they had quite recently originated from the second story (upper room) room where they had eaten their last supper together.

Jesus had cautioned them of their shortcoming in face of risk; even Peter would deny him there multiple times before the sun would arise the following morning.

Judas had gone on his insidious mission; the other disciples were now to observe Jesus Christ's anguish and his betrayal. Eight of them were advised to sit close to the passageway of the garden, however they were not kept in obscurity about our Lord's plan to meet the horrible test; by supplication he would submit himself completely to his Father. The suggestion is the they ought to supplicate (pray) as well.

The three disciples who had been advantaged to witness the transfiguration - Peter, James, and John - were called to go with Jesus more profoundly into the garden. They saw how Jesus was overwhelmed with "distress" and "trouble."

These two words are hard to interpret; they express the most extreme level of unbounded repulsiveness and suffering. In this difficult hour he required the presence of his three most confided in companions.

In his humanity the Lord Jesus was defenseless against indistinguishable feelings of dread and distresses from we are. He was in each respect... tempted as we seem to be" (Heb. 4:15). The extraordinary trial of this hour was confronting the rejection of men, the physical torment, and the horrendous nervousness of physical affliction, however we know nothing of bearing someone else's wrongdoing (sin) and judgment. In view of his own flawlessness (perfection, sinless), this was even more hard for Jesus to manage.

Jesus acknowledged to Peter, James, and John the profundities of his own anguish. His distress was caused both by what awaited him and by the sinfulness of men. He had sobbed over the city of Jerusalem.

Now his distress gets abusive, "even to death." It is as though he were to die before his time under this heap of mental and spiritual agony and misery. Here means that the amount he suffered even before the cross. History records the people who have died of sorrow. The Lord Jesus Christ moved toward this sort of involvement with the garden.

At this basic point he advised the three disciples to watch, that is, to remain conscious, to keep alert. He was not searching for protectors, but for comfort and strength.

"Keep me company as I suffer" is the significance here. It did him good to have them next to him. We as a whole know the security and strength that originated from having companions share our deepest suffering.

His Prayer For Deliverance
(vv. 35, 36)

The disciples knew Jesus was a man of supplication (prayer). It was not astonishing to them that he had gone to Gethsemane for this reason. This was no unexpected drive, no supplication incited by a crisis. Jesus walked in whole partnership with his heavenly Father; he went through hours in prayer as a normal habit.

Every so often the gospel authors uncover the substance of Jesus Christ's petitions, however in no extraordinary detail, with the exception of John 17. Here, Mark reveals to us what Jesus was supplicating about, and afterward incorporates the particular words he used to make his solicitation known to God.

The awful strain of confronting the cross bore in on Christ, so he mulled over an exit from it, "that, in the event that it were conceivable, the hour may go from him." "The hour," obviously, is a reference to his pending capture, trial, conviction, and execution on the cross.

Jesus Christ's petition in v. 36 uncovers both his humanity and his complete submission to his Father's will and plan. He addressed God in the certainty that he could deliver him, that he could produce some other solution for the issue of the world's sin. "All things are possible to thee" shows an incomparable confidence in the hour of preliminary (trial).

Such a faith is the bedrock of petition. There is no reason for asking in the event that we don't trust God is almighty and all-powerful the supreme ruler of the universe.

The solicitation of Jesus was explicit: "remove this cup from me." What does "the cup" speak to here? It represents the anguish of physical torment, but additionally for the loathsomeness of spiritual misery, which no person can completely appreciate.

Numerous people have confronted approaching martydom with fortitude, but none of them has suffered being made sin (II Cor. 5:21). On the cross he who was pure was presented to the divine judgment on transgression (sin). In the garden Jesus confronted the truth of what it would intend to taste in the entirety of its harshness that death which is the wages of sin.

Christ's words, "Yet not what I will, however what thou wilt," take us to the peak of his Gethsemane experience. If there was no other path separated from the cross to verify the salvation of the world, Jesus was happy to acknowledge the cross.

Here we see his genuine human will, unmistakable from, however accommodating to, the desire of his Father. In this he uncovered the example for all who might be Christians. Self-will must go; God's will must be acknowledged, and accepted regardless.

In this promise to the Father's will Jesus went unalterably to Calvary. The triumph of the cross was in truth won in this petition in Gethsemane. Satan brought sin and death into the world by affirming his will against God (Isa. 14:13, 14); Jesus brought our salvation by presenting his will to God. For us, respecting God's will likewise brings victory, however demanding our own specific manner prompts rout.

(Request that companions offer encounters in which they confronted the issue: Shall it be my will or God's? What thwarts us from making the total give up? How had Jesus set himself up for this responsibility? Work out, what "this cup" signifies as far as some current condition. How might you minister to somebody whom you know is opposing God's will?)

Jesus Christ's Total Suffering
(Mark 15:33-39 NIV)

We don't have the foggiest idea to what extent Jesus anguished in petition. Evidently it was not exceptionally long. He before long stirred his resting (sleeping) disciples and proceeded to confront Judas and the officials. His petition of duty fortified Jesus to confront them; he neither fled nor approached the heavenly angels to destroy his adversaries.

Paul says of Jesus, "And being found in human form he humbled himself and became obedient unto death, even death on a cross" (Phil. 2:8). These verses in Mark portray the last snapshots of the most significant, critical death that has ever happened in history.

His Cry On The Cross
(vv. 33, 34)

Darkness encompassed Jerusalem from early afternoon until 3 P.M. Jesus had been crucified at 9 A.M., so his cry came after he persevered through six hours of horrendous torment. Mark and Matthew record his words in Aramaic, the basic language of the day, and afterward give them in Greek. What do they mean?

As a result of the unique relationship in the Godhead among Father and Son we may never, on this side of glory, have the option to get a handle on the profundity of feeling behind these words.

Our Lord's cry doesn't simply mirror an inclination that he was being forsaken on the cross, but they show the awful reality that right then and there - as he bore the transgressions (sins) of the world in his own body - God really walked out (turned his back) on his Son and abandoned him.

This takes us to the core of the sacrifice, Christ's substitutionary death for our benefit. To be forsaken on the cross was a need for Jesus. Since God can not look upon sin (Hab. 1:13), he shrouded (hid) his face, so to speak, when our sin was set upon his perfect, sinless Son.

In actuality, Jesus was forsaken with the goal that we may never be (Heb. 13:5). This was the supreme theological actuality that caused such a cry from our suffering Savior on the cross. Our sin made him suffer the nails and the lance, but also the deserting (abandonment) by his Father.

The Crowd's Reaction
(vv. 35, 36)

Some of the people watching thought Jesus was calling for Elijah. It was assumed that the great prophet would one day return. What preferred time over now, to safeguard the person who professed to be God's Son. Someone else lifted a sponge loaded with vinegar to the perishing form. Those present couldn't comprehend that Christ's anguish was substantially more than physical.

Jesus Christ's Last Words
(vv. 37, 38)

The LOUD cry was, "Father, into thy hands I commit my spirit!" (Luke 23:46) and, "It is finished" (John 19:30). None of the journalists state that Jesus died. The loud cry toward the end shows that Jesus died not from common causes or weariness. His death was willful and in this way exceptional.

He really surrendered his life, as he said he would (John 10:15-18). He did this before any physical reason realized his dying; he did it right now based on his very own preference. Most exploited people executed on the cross waited for a day or more; this is the thing that made torturous killing so awful. On account of Jesus, Pilate asked why Jesus had died unexpectedly early (v. 44).

God connoted the significance of the cross for the Jews in the tearing of the sanctuary window ornament (the curtain). Later on, numerous clerics accepted (Acts 6:7). Following quite a while of worship in the tabernacle and the temple, in which the Holy of Holies had been shut to all aside from the consecrated cleric on the Day of Atonement, presently the best approach to God was open for all, a new and living path through Jesus Christ himself (Heb. 10:19-22).

The Roman Centurion's Testimony
(v. 39)

This Roman warrior, stationed where he could see all that had occurred, was dazzled by the way of Jesus Christ's passing. Despite the fact that his words may not reflect total comprehension now, he remains as the first among numerous who down through the ages would be attracted to Christ by the power of his sacrifice on the cross. (What have you guaranteed for yourself because of Christ's death for you? What personal needs and issues do you presently have that could be met by setting aside some effort to think about what occurred on Calvary?).

End: Thank God that Jesus persevered through the passing we deserved! "For Christ additionally died for sins once for all, the noble for the indecent, that he may carry us to God... He himself bore our sins in his body on the tree, that we may die to sin and live to righteousness. By his wounds you have been healed" (I Peter 3:18; 2:24 RSV).

Chapter Nineteen

Jesus Lives
(Mark 15:42-16:8 KJV)

"He has risen" is the best news the world has ever heard. The words must be said of the Lord Jesus Christ. In this way, the Christian has hope to offer the world. The expectation of the world isn't the resurrection of spring blooms, however the triumph at Easter.

Their festival depends on the reality of the unfilled tomb. Of all the world's great religious pioneers, only Jesus Christ abandoned a vacant tomb. Only he became alive once again.

At Easter we not only think back to the holy angel's brilliant declaration, we likewise take a look at the present truth of Christ in the lives of his own and at the conviction of his coming later on. Our present and future hope is tied down in the reality of his resurrection from the dead.

As the messenger Paul noted, "In the event that Christ has not been raised, at that point our proclaiming is futile and your confidence is futile" (I Cor. 15:14). Everything pivots upon the reality of Christ's returning to life once more. Without that, there is no affirmation of his divinity, no confirmation of our forgiveness, and no confirmation of everlasting life.

Easter is unmistakably more than the retelling of an antiquated legend; Easter pronounces that Jesus Christ is alive now and anyone can go into a personal relationship with him. Without that faith relationship, one's life will undoubtedly end in misery and judgment. Knowing Jesus Christ today offers peace and hope.

The world of nature at springtime lets us know of fresh starts (new beginnings). Any person can make a fresh start with Jesus Christ whenever, on the grounds that Christ became alive once again. He lives in our souls by faith, which is similarly as genuine as the new blossoms pushing through the ground.

This lesson offers us a chance to know the realities of Jesus Christ's resurrection and to apply those realities to needs in our lives.

The Burial Of Jesus
(Mark 15:42-47 KJV)

No funeral service courses of action had been made for Jesus. His companions had dispersed and it would be too dangerous to even consider showing any distinguishing proof with the unfortunate casualty now. Jesus had been executed at the request of a wailing crowd motivated by Israel's strict religious leaders. With the exception of the gatekeepers (guards) at Golgotha, nobody had any further obligation in this issue.

But one man ventured forward to see that Jesus had a respectable entombment. God had his man arranged for this consequence. Joseph would not allow any further insults to the body of God's Son. He strikingly willingly volunteered to bury the Savior.

Joseph Asked For The Body Of Jesus
(vv. 42, 43)

Jesus held tight the cross from 9 o'clock in the first part of the day until 3 o'clock toward the evening, when he died. It was Friday, the day preceding the sabbath, Saturday. Friday was designated "the day of Preparation" since it was the day the Jews arranged for their sabbath observances. The sabbath started at dusk on Friday.

Jewish law didn't allow a dead body to stay unburied after nightfall (sundown). Had not Jesus' body been claimed it would have been tossed into a typical pit. Hence, at night Joseph of Arimathea took boldness and chose to turn out openly and request the body of Jesus.

Certain critical realities about Joseph are noted. His town of origin, Arimathea, has not been found, but obviously he lived in Jerusalem for quite a while. There, he became "a respected member of the council," that is, the Sanhedrin, or ruling body of Jewish elders.

All things considered, he partook in the trial of Jesus, however he casted a ballot against his conviction and judgment (Luke 23:51). Luke calls him "a good and righteous man" (23:50), while John distinguishes Joseph as a secret disciple (19:38), secret because he feared the Jews.

Mark portrays Joseph's faith as far as his "searching for the kingdom of God." This implies he accepted the Old Testament predictions and acknowledged Christ as the Messiah in fulfillment of these prophecies. Such a confession would, obviously, chafe the Jewish pioneers, who had rejected Christ's claims to be the Son of God.

Be that as it may, a significant change came over Joseph following the death of Jesus. Maybe Joseph was so dazzled by the manner in which Jesus confronted his persecutors and suffered torturous killing that he chose to turn out strongly in favor of Christ. He "took courage" and went to Pilate to request the body of Jesus. he was never again a secret disciple.

The dangers were impressive, on the grounds that both Pilate and the Jewish elders could disapprove of Joseph's boldness. There was no chance he could shroud what he needed to do. So his affection for Jesus conquered his feelings of trepidation. Obviously, his vote against denouncing Christ would have made him think, but what he did now was a progressively gallant act.

Faith demands courage. There is no simple time to accept and confess Christ. The people who are against Christ and the people who love to ridicule believers appear to be constantly aware of any outward declaration for Christ.

Again and again, Christians are quiet, secret disciples. They neglect to take advantage of the opportunity to speak out, to witness, to state straightforwardly that they are Christians. They fear conceivable criticism and trouble. Only a strong faith in Christ can conquer such weaknesses (cowardice).

Pilate Granted The Body To Joseph
(vv. 44, 45)

Pilate presumably was shocked when Joseph showed up before him. He more likely than not believed that the entirety of Christ's companions were too scared to even think about reappearing unexpectedly early. Be that as it may, his fundamental concern was whether Jesus was dead; normally the casualties of execution waited for twenty-four hours or more before they died.

The centurion announced that Jesus had as of now died, so Pilate conceded Joseph's solicitation. Obviously there was nobody around from among the Jewish elders to meddle now. They may have encouraged Pilate to refuse. In any case, Pilate's giving of consent for entombment was as per general Roman methodology in such cases.

Joseph Buried Jesus
(v. 46)

The internment of Jesus involved a significant spot in the doctrines of the early church since it demonstrated the truth of his death (cf. I Cor. 15:3, 4).

Jesus was not buried with the resplendent trappings of today; there was no costly coffin.

In those days graves were not dug from underneath the ground and secured with flowers.

Joseph essentially enveloped the assemblage of Jesus by a cloth cover (linen) and laid him in a tomb that had been cut out of rock. Matthew adds the fact that this was Joseph's "own new tomb" (27:60). Jewish graves were caverns, normal or man-made, in the sides of slopes, huge enough for an individual to walk in.

By and large, only the wealthy could bear the cost of a private tomb. Before the tomb having a place with a rich family there were commonly a vestibule open to the air, at that point a low passageway. Inside the square chamber there was a place for the body, either cut somewhere in the range of seven feet into the stone, or the long way three feet down, with a low curve over it.

To bury Jesus not only required mental fortitude with respect to Joseph but in addition sacrifice. Surrendering his own tomb was expensive. John says the tomb was situated "in the garden" (19:41).

Since the time of Constantine, the customary tomb of Christ has been the one above which towers the vault of the Church of the Holy Sepulcher. Be that as it may, a few researchers accept the entombment occurred in the alleged "Garden Tomb" outside the old wall of Jerusalem.

Subsequent to setting Christ's body in the tomb, Joseph "rolled a stone against the entryway of the tomb." The entryway of the tomb may be rectangular and of strong stone, with a spine fitting into a socket for a hinge, or it may be a round and hollow stone which abounded in a depression to one side or left of the opening.

In certain tombs there were customary entryways of stone upheld by pivots, against which a stone was moved for further insurance. It is beyond the realm of imagination to expect to state without a doubt what sort of an entryway Joseph had on his tomb.

The Women Noted The Place
(v. 47)

Two of the women who saw the torturous killing (crucifixion) (v. 40) additionally noted where Joseph had buried Jesus. We will see their purpose for this in the accompanying verses. (Who do you think ought to have buried Jesus? Why? What upsides and downsides do you think Joseph said something in his psyche before he chose to move toward Pilate?

The Resurrection Of Jesus
(Mark 16:1-8 KJV)

These verses record the main events of Christ's resurrection day. Through and through, his post-resurrection ministry incorporated forty days (Acts 1:3). The focal figures in this entry are the women and the angel. Afterward, obviously, the disciples and Jesus himself figured in the energizing developments. Actually, in the event that you needed to choose one single word to describe the disposition of those early hours, it would be excitement.

The Women Wanted To Anoint Him
(vv. 1, 2)

Joseph and Nicodemus had bound the assemblage of Jesus "in linen cloths with the spices" (John 19:40), however obviously the women either didn't have the foggiest idea about this, or else they felt the Lord's body had not been appropriately treated.

The "spices" were sweet-smelling herbs that were blended in with oil. Perhaps Joseph and Nicodemus had done their work hastily, however regardless of whether they had done the treating in the most ideal manner, the women could in any case have gone on their mission to the grave, just out of profound love for Christ.

These women had pursued the Lord wholeheartedly; they needed to show their devotion by tending to his dormant body.

They are recognized as Mary Magdalene, that is, of the town of Magdala on the Sea of Galilee (Jesus had cast seven devils from her, Luke 8:2); Mary the mother of James and Joses (cf. 15:40, 47); and Salome, the spouse of Zebedee, the mother of the followers James and John.

At the point when the sabbath was past, that is, after twilight (sundown) on Saturday, they purchased the spices, but they held up until first light (dawn) to go to the grave site.

They Worried About How To Move The Stone (vv. 3, 4)

The prompt obstruction to the fulfillment of their assignment of devotion was the enormous stone that banned the passageway to the tomb. Clearly they had considered the issue previously, however it didn't dissuade them from heading off to the tomb.

These were women of colossal faith and mental fortitude; they were not scared of potential results, nor did their absence of solidarity to move the stone trouble them.

Apparently their question isn't one of uncertainty but of faith. They proceeded in assurance that God would give somebody to do what they required. Their solitary inquiry was who.

Barely had they raised it among themselves when they got their answer. Envision their extraordinary amazement when they saw that the tomb had been opened. God knew their faith and he had sent a heavenly angel to move back the stone.

The holy angel opened the passageway to the tomb not to open the route for the risen Lord, however for the women, the disciples who came later, and the Roman watchmen (cf. Matt. 28:4). The Romans would need to realize that their power was not sufficiently able to frustrate the plan of God.

In any case, the open tomb was fundamentally to serve the disciples, whose faith was so powerless (weak) as of now. As Thomas was to expose his fingers in the injuries (wounds) of Christ's body, so the disciples were to investigate with their eyes the open grave, so as to be convinced by their faculties that the executed, dead, and buried Savior had to be sure arisen and was alive.

They Entered The Tomb And Were Surprised To See An Angel
(v. 5)

The unwavering, valiant women didn't have the foggiest idea how the stone had been moved back, but they endured and headed inside. Inside they met "a young man," that is, a holy angel (cf. Matt.

28:2). He wore "a white robe," symbolizing the immaculateness and light of paradise's brilliance.

Generally, angels in the biblicial records showed up as a man; only in the Old Testament records do they show up in this clothing.

Seeing the heavenly attendant flabbergasted the women. The word utilized here incorporates both amazement and fear. Indeed, they had faith, but we can't anticipate that they should enter the tomb and afterward observe this weird individual without their being overpowered with amazement and fear.

The Angel Announced Jesus Christ's Resurrection And Told The Women To Tell The Disciples (vv. 6, 7)

The heavenly angel originally consoled the women and afterward attempted to quiet their feelings of dread. That was their immediate need. At that point he responded to their implicit inquiries and revealed to them what had occurred. The body of Jesus was not there; he welcomed them to inspect the tomb.

The explanation the body was not there was on the grounds that Jesus had become alive once again. The angel's words were a declaration of the reality, not a depiction of the occasion. Nobody saw Jesus return to life and leave the tomb; nobody has had the option to depict the resurrection procedure in physical terms.

In any case, the obvious certainties of history are: the tomb was vacant and Jesus appeared to his disciples and many different onlookers (cf. I Cor. 15:5, 6). His resurrection body had the recognizable characteristics of the body preceding his death, but it was an alternate body, since he could go through entryways (cf. John 20:19, 26).

The angel's declaration was straightforward; "he is risen" truly signifies "he was awakened." This was simply the result he had anticipated ordinarily. We are astonished that nobody, not in any case these women anticipated it, but we can't be excessively critical of them. What number of us would have believed under these conditions?

Numerous individuals today won't accept the resurrection of Christ. Various hypotheses have been developed to clarify it away. However, as Professor Edmund Wolf comments, "The word angel appeals to our confidence more than these silly devices of unsanctified reason...A church in which the living forces of eternal life are at work has not grown out of a corpse. It rests upon one who has conquered death and is alive forever more."

The proof for the resurrection reaches out past the historical backdrop of the vacant tomb and the declaration of the people who saw Jesus alive. It stretches out to our very own time in the existence and survival of the church.

The resurrection is additionally confirmed by the abstract understanding of Christian believers: the peace, joy, and hope they know because of the risen Christ within themselves.

The holy messenger (angel) likewise had a commission for the women. Clearly the women inspected the unfilled tomb, at that point the heavenly angel guided them to tell the disciples and Peter that Jesus would meet them in Galilee. These women were to be the first errand people (messengers) of the tremendous Easter announcement.

As a result, it was an exceptional greeting to see the risen Lord himself. They were not welcome to see a phantom (ghost), or a "spiritually raised" person, but the real person and body of Jesus Christ.

The heavenly angel also reminded the women that Jesus had found faith among the humble and the troubled; in Galilee he had called the twelve; so in Galilee he gathered his scattered flock around him again. This post-resurrection appearance in Galilee is most likely the time when Jesus was seen by in excess of 500 brethren at once.

The Women Were Overcome With Fear (v. 8)

The women wavered among faith and unfaith. They likely wanted to believe the magnificent declaration of the angel, however they were too overwhelmed with fear and shock. As much as they may want to, despite everything they can't believe what has occurred.

It is conceivable that they were basically too overwhelmed by stun to say anything, but it is almost certain they were similarly as delayed as the disciples to have faith in the resurrection of Christ. Be that as it may, they slowly recuperated and faithfully reported what had occurred (cf. Luke 24:22).

The voyage of the women began in affection (love) for Jesus Christ and ended in dismay (fright), as well we might have felt had we been there, but that isn't the end of the Easter story.

The risen Christ now offers hope, joy, and eternal life to all who will trust in him. Jesus Christ is the life and he gives life.

(What do you appreciate most about the women? Is there something about their character you could imitate? Why does it matter to you whether Jesus is dead or alive? What might be the fate if the angel had not said, "He has risen"? Rundown three changes throughout your life achieved by Jesus Christ's resurrection.)

End: Jesus Christ lives at the right hand of the Father in glory and in each Christian's heart. Easter helps us again to remember the Father's power and his love.

The apostle Paul supplicated that every Christian may understand the significance of that power (Eph. 1:19, 20 KJV). If we give ourselves to the risen Christ, he can work out that power for our needs and cares.

Chapter Twenty

Jesus Assures His Disciples
(Surprised By Joy)
(Luke 24:13-16, 25-35 KJV)

MANY PEOPLE ON THE planet today act like the two disciples walking to Emmaus: they are continuing on ahead as if Jesus Christ had not been raised from the dead. 2,000 years after the occasion they are unaffected by it; they have no close to home involvement in the living Christ.

For them, Christ is consigned to the futile services of religion. He might be a noteworthy person throughout the entire existence of religion, however he has no affect on their way of living. To the extent they are concerned, he should in any case be in the grave.

Indeed, even the people who make some calling of religious faith know close to nothing or nothing of the indwelling truth of Jesus Christ. Their faith incorporates custom and statement of faith, but no power, no reality, no life-changing dynamic.

That it is so appalling to have this power accessible and not utilize it! Jesus Christ knocks at the entryways of the hearts of people, but they won't welcome him into their lives. This is on the grounds that they need to keep control of their lives; they don't need an "outside power" in charge.

As a matter of fact, surrender to Jesus is costly - it costs you your self-but it is the only way to have access to his power. With such a large number of personal, national, and world-wide needs around us, it is basic that Christians share the truth of the risen Christ.

He was strong enough to become alive once more (rise from the grave), to defeat sin and death; thusly, we can confide in him to be strong enough to address our issues, to vanquish our feelings of fears and anxieties, and to meet our needs.

This lesson shows both Christ's accessibility and the need to have one's eyes opened in regards to who he truly is. While people are grabbing aimlessly for answers, Christians must affirm the possibility of a personal walk with the Lord Jesus.

The Perplexity Of The Men
(Luke 24:13-16 KJV)

Easter should been a period of rejoicing and festivity, yet rather - in light of the fact that its centrality was not gotten a handle on - it turned into a period of perplexity, disarray, frustration, and misery. We meet two men who endured this thwarted expectation on the first Easter day. This Sunday - one week after Easter - we also can find people who are worrying about unrelieved concerns and issues since they have not by faith confided in the risen Christ.

They Discussed The Crucifixion
(vv. 13, 14)

The time and the place are revealed by Luke, however just the name of one of them, Cleopas (v. 18). "That very day" alludes obviously to the day of Christ's resurrection. The hour of day likely was late evening, since they before long came to Emmaus, seven miles northwest of Jerusalem. These men were not of the Twelve, however were from the whole body of the disciples. At the point when they returned to Jerusalem, they went to meet "the eleven" (v. 33).

There is no true information accessible either about Cleopas or his anonymous partner. Maybe Luke might not have known the name of the other person. Among the conjectures: Luke himself.

They talked "pretty much every one of these things that had occurred," which means obviously the torturous killing (crucifixion) of Jesus. When Jesus asked them what they were discussing later on (vv. 17-24), it became evident they were accomplishing more than practicing the realities.

They were truly upset by the disappointment of Jesus to "redeem Israel," that is, to set Israel from the domain of Rome. They were persuaded that Jesus "was a mighty prophet," however they couldn't accommodate that with his death before their own chief priests and rulers.

To add to their perplexity, they had heard reports of the vacant tomb, they got the report of the messenger (angel) that Jesus was alive. What could this mean?

Plainly these men were genuine disciples, but befuddled. With them it was anything but an instance of no longer of any concern. Their musings still fixated on Jesus; their preservation was about him, even on the third day after his execution.

Despite the fact that they had not had enough faith to believe he would become alive once again from the dead, these men had an essential commitment to Christ as their one and all. If they could, they would still like to be with the one whom they last saw on Good Friday. Their craving was destined to be met.

Jesus Walked With Them, But They Didn't Know It (vv. 15, 16)

As the men were charmed in their discussion, Jesus followed along and went along with them. Likely he came up from behind, but the men demonstrated nothing unexpected. Evidently it was standard in those days to enable complete aliens to join your gathering.

"Jesus himself moved close" in view of his love and compassion. He had promised, "For where two or three are gathered in my name, there am I in the midst of them" (Matt. 18:20). These men had done nothing exceptional to merit Christ's presence. They had a profound need that they themselves didn't completely get it. Only the presence of Christ could help them.

In one sense, these two sheep in their misery had meandered away from the group. The Good Shepherd followed them to fortify them in their shortcoming and to take them back to the fold. He does likewise for us today; he gravitates toward in the midst of demoralization and uncertainty.

These men didn't perceive the person walking with them as being the Lord Jesus himself. Maybe it was a direct result of new attire; some have thought their despondency was so incredible and their faith so little that they couldn't get a handle on what his identity was. Whatever the outward reason, for their need, plainly God had an essential spiritual plan at the top of the priority list in mind in shielding them from perceiving Jesus.

They expected to see who Jesus truly was, significantly more than thinking of him as an alleged savior of Israel who fizzled. They expected to see the teaching of their own Scripture about him; they expected to perceive how their encounters fit the Scripture.

Jesus pursued a similar guideline he had taught: a person couldn't see until he had first believed. Jesus consistently called for commitment first. "If any man's will is to do his (God's) will, he shall know..." (John 7:17 KJV). So he said to Thomas,

"Blessed are the people who have not seen but believe" (John 20:29 KJV).

(What questions and frustrations do you face today? Have you conversed with others about them? Have you welcomed Jesus into your discussion? For what reason do you think Jesus walked with these men? What help do you get from the way that he did?)

Jesus Christ's Bible Teaching
(Luke 24:25-27 NIV)

In the intervening verses we have the answer of the men to Christ's inquiry concerning their discussion. From the outset they were too dismal to even think about talking increasingly about it, however then Cleopas clarified their subject and their emotions.

Jesus responded such that probably stunned them. He didn't continue with some considerate comment: he censured them and afterward he showed them the scriptural viewpoint on these occasions - at the same time not revealing his identity to them.

Jesus Rebuke Of Their Ignorance
(vv. 25, 26)

For what reason did Jesus talk so strongly, yet affectionately to these men? Was their blunder so incredible? Is it true that they were blameworthy of some extraordinary sin? Not the things that we regularly consider as transgression (sin). However, their carelessness was basic: they didn't accept "all that the prophets" had spoken.

The words "slow of heart" truly signify "void of mind," without intelligence. Their comprehension was injured. Why? Since they had decided to accept the predictions that secured the glory of the messianic realm, however they had disregarded or had would not acknowledge the predictions that discussed Messiah as the Lamb of God prompted the butcher.

They more likely than not had some information of Christ's torturous killing (crucifixion). To them, with regards to the Greeks, the cross was silliness.

Maybe they thought they knew the prophets, yet their alleged information vanished despite darkness and troubles.

Their hearts clung to the glories of a messianic realm; amidst their ran expectations they were not able see that the topple they had always wanted ought to have driven them to reality of Scripture.

Subsequent to accusing them of accepting just part of the prophetic message, Jesus focused in on the vital point. He got some information about the need of Messiah's misery.

This inquiry is a declaration of what is going to pursue. Keep in mind, as of now he is as yet an obscure outsider. How might you feel about somebody uncovering your absence of confidence and comprehension?

Truly, the prophets particularly, even minutely, had depicted the sufferings of Christ; just "fools, slow of heart" neglected to observe them. Indeed, what had insulted them and broken their faith was the surest confirmation that this Jesus of Nazareth was the person who ought to redeem Israel.

Maybe Jesus had said to them, "The very things that you let me know are reasons for your questions are the trademark characteristics of the Christ." It was vital for Jesus so to suffer, or he would not have been the Lord's Messiah.

The exact thing that Jesus needed to do, if he somehow happened to satisfy the Scriptures and execute his mission, what was confused to these men.

Suffering and death didn't come to pass for Jesus unintentionally; what had happened was by the unceasing counsel of the eternal God. The prophets were roused to anticipate Christ's suffering in light of the fact that God wanted to save the world only through a suffering Messiah.

Be that as it may, his suffering was not the end of God's plan. Jesus clarified a definitive reason: to "go into his glory." Suffering and glory are intimately connected.

Jesus Interpretation Of Scripture
(v. 27)

How could these men answer the stranger's pointed inquiry? Was their answer yes or no? From this side of the cross and the vacant tomb, we state yes. Be that as it may, the sufferings of Christ at that point and now are a hindrance (cf. Matt. 16:22 NIV). His sufferings structure the time when the gradualness of faith most displays itself. In this manner, these men required a Bible lesson, or a Bible supplemental class.

How might you want to think about under Jesus? These men did. Jesus gave them how the Old Testament related to himself. That is the thing that we ought to consistently search for in the Old Testament: the lessons about Christ, his torment and glory.

The Bible itself is our position, our authority; it is there we see the need of Christ's dying for us. He died for our transgressions (sins); in the event that he had not languished over us, we would at present be under judgment and condemnation.

(For what reason is it difficult to accept God's standard of suffering before glory? What advantages do you want from Christ's coming? Is it true that they are in accordance with Scriptures? What amount of one's absence of spiritual development can be credited to numbness of Scripture?)

Jesus Christ's Revelation Of Himself
(Luke 24:28-31 KJV)

We don't have a clue to what extent this Bible lesson endured, however it more likely than not been over an hour or two. Night was coming and some idea must be given to friendliness and lodging. In this setting of ordinary prerequisites the Lord Jesus unfurled the great truth about himself.

Jesus Revealed Himself In
The Breaking Of Bread
(vv. 30, 31)

There was a peculiar inversion here, yet this pursued the example of the entire scene. This stranger had meandered into a profound talk, yet he offered the exercise and the responses; he assumed responsibility for the discussion and made genuine allegations against his friends.

Next, they welcomed him to remain with them, yet as opposed to acting like the visitor he acted like the host. Here at this basic supper, as in the basic walk together, the Lord Jesus guided occasions to draw out reality with regards to himself.

Accepting the job of host, he took the bread, that is, in the job as master of the house, he expressed gratefulness before the supper. At that point he served it.

This, incidentally, was not a model of the Lord's Supper, or Communion service. These two men were not in the Upper Room with Jesus when he established the Lord's Supper. Likewise, the words "blessed and broke it" happen at common suppers (cf. Luke 9:16 KJV).

At that point something surprising occurred: "their eyes were opened and they perceived" Jesus. Quickly, he vanished. The circumstance of v. 16 was totally switched. Once more, we don't have the exact physical reason that God used to open their eyes.

Was there something about his supplication that blended them, or did they see proof of the execution in his body? Whatever it was, it was quick. In a minute, every one of the pieces fit together. In any case, they were not to make the most of his presence any more.

Maybe God was going to test their faith again. They couldn't stick to Christ's physical presence for help. Their faith would need to help them through.

Christ's post-revival appearances normally were of brief span. Without a doubt, this was to assemble faith in his believers.

The Bible doesn't tell how Jesus showed up and returned after his resurrection. This was one of various abrupt, undetectable withdrawals and appearances. Christ's body was celebrated, so he had the ability to show up and vanish freely.

For what reason did Jesus reveal himself now? Once more, it was a direct result of his empathy. He reacted to the requirements of these men, not just by gravitating toward them out and about, yet additionally by completely revealing himself.

In the event that we set aside effort to ponder his teaching, and in the event that we welcome him to "stay with us," we can be certain that we will get a handle on the truth of his presence.

The Certainty Of The Men
(Luke 24:32-35 NIV)

Perplexity offered approach to confirmation; despair offered approach to euphoria. Something gigantic had happened to these down and out disciples. They had another euphoria to impart to their brethren in Jerusalem, so they wasted through no time in coming back to give their report.

Their Burning Hearts
(v. 32)

These men didn't pose rationalistic inquires about Christ's unexpected vanishing. They could have lost their spiritual opportunity by discussing the "how" of what had simply occurred. Rather, they thought back and confessed a genuine spiritual conviction.

The Holy Spirit had been grinding away while Jesus showed them the significance of the prophecies. His work was real that it made their hearts be set burning (aflame).

The spiritual spark that lit the fire in their hearts had been Christ's inquiry (v. 26). Their bluntness was transformed into comprehension and enthusiasm. Compelling feelings (strong emotions) are depicted by the symbolism of fire. So today we speak of people being "on fire" for Jesus.

This fire is more than feeling, notwithstanding. These men ascribed it to Christ's conversion and teaching, "while he opened to us the scriptures." True spiritual vitality will consistently grow out of the time we provide for the study of God's Word.

Their Witness To The Brethren
(vv. 33-35)

The men didn't delay; they couldn't head to sleep and rest on such sublime, glorious news. Despite the fact that it was night - and evening time travel was deceptive - they rushed back to Jerusalem. They realized where to locate the eleven and different believers.

Without a moment's delay, they were told the updates on Christ's resurrection and his appearance to Peter. Thusly, they shared what Jesus had accomplished for them out and about and "in the breaking of bread." Thus the snippets of data about the resurrection began to fall together, and the Christians were built up in their trust in Jesus.

He was by and large consistent with his promise. Alongside is teaching about his death, the Lord Jesus had predicted his resurrection. Now, regardless of spiritual bluntness among his disciples, he showed them and led them along lovingly and calmly (patiently).

(Request that somebody share how they came to recognize the truth about Christ. What snags keep people from recognizing him today? How

Dr. John Thomas Wylie

might you help carry the presence of Christ to them? What part does Bible study play in increasing a knowledge on Jesus Christ? How might you assist somebody with knowing him that way? How might you portray a Christian whose heart is burning for Christ? For what reason aren't more Christians like that?)

These men moved from uncertainty to faith because they increased in a personal knowledge about Jesus Christ. He gravitated toward to them and translated the Scriptures, and their hearts were set aflame. He keeps on showing himself today, not exclusively to move our faith, but in addition to send us forward as witnesses to truth that he lives.

Chapter Twenty-One

Jesus Commissions His Followers
(Luke 24:44-53 KJV)

THE OVERALL MISSION OF the church was inspired by the commission of the Lord Jesus Christ. The Israelites of old were to be a witness to the one true God among the nations, but as time wore on the religion of Israel turned out to be progressively thin and nationalistic. Gentiles were detested and evaded at every possible opportunity.

Jesus Christ showed up on the scene and he obviously brought a saving message and hope for the whole world. He reproached the Jews for their customary neutrality and he clarified that God was demonstrating his love for all people. John the baptizer saw this significant truth when he cried of Jesus, "Behold, the Lamb of God, who takes away the sin of the world!" (John 1:29 NASB).

Be that as it may, regardless of its worldwide mandate, the church has now and again in its history slipped by into disobedience and indifference. For the first three centuries of the Christian period there were extraordinary steps of advancement, as the Christians brought the gospel into Europe, Africa, and Asia. A few researchers think the gospel likewise was preached in China.

In any case, when Christianity was perceived by the Romans, a specific unwinding set in. The cutting edge advance of the gospel started in the nineteenth century, in spite of the fact that there were infrequent periods before that when a few people broke out of the accepted patterns of complacency.

In the last one hundred years of clans and factions everywhere throughout the world have heard the uplifting news of Jesus for the first time. God has blessed the preaching of his word and churches have been established in about each corner of the globe.

This is a period of enormous harvest for Christ; a few researchers gauge that in excess of 50,000 individuals consistently (every day) are converted to faith in Jesus Christ. However the total populace is developing by about 150,000 consistently (every day), so the assignment of obeying Jesus Christ's commission stays upon all Christians and churches. This lesson will assist us with understanding the basic truths of his commission.

Jesus Fulfilled The Scriptures
(Luke 24:44, 45 KJV)

After Jesus appeared to the travelers on the way to Emmaus, he went to where the believers were gathered in Jerusalem. He "stood among them," however they were startled, agitated, and puzzled by his abrupt appearance.

They thought they were seeing an apparition, however Jesus welcomed them to deal with his resurrected body. To demonstrate further that he was not a spirit, he ate a bit of cooked fish (broiled).

Bit by bit reality of Christ's resurrection from the grave unfolded on these people. "Despite everything they questioned for satisfaction." His presence with them was unrealistic. In any case, as they started to acknowledge the way that the one standing before them was in reality the Lord Jesus Christ, he practiced the essential actualities of Scripture for them.

It is a miracle that Jesus didn't relinquish them in their unbelief. Were these the ones to whom he was going to give a world-wide mission the spread of the faith?

What were their capabilities for such a huge errand? They were not prepared scholastically; they had no political or military aptitudes; they had next to no to offer.

More awful, they had fled their leader in his time of most noteworthy trial and now they wouldn't accept what he himself had shown them - that he would become alive once again. However the Lord Jesus didn't abandon them.

By then it resembled a horrible mistake to proceed with his commission to these individuals, but Jesus showed again that his wisdom is superior to our own and furthermore that his love is patient and forgiving. That is the sort of love we can rely on today.

Regularly, Christians feel insufficient for what God needs them to do. They would lean toward not to receive his commission for a particular duty. However, that is an ideal opportunity to think back on this occasion. God's plan was culminated, not on the grounds that the human instruments were satisfactory in themselves, but since his insight and love were adequate for every one of their needs.

Everything Must Be Fulfilled
(v. 44)

Paul summarized the gospel by saying that Jesus died, was buried, and rose once more "as per the scriptures" (I Cor. 15:3, 4 NIV). All through the four accounts (four gospels), the authors clarify the occasions throughout Christ's life as such: "This was to fulfill what the Lord had spoken by the prophet."

His whole life and ministry were rooted in the Old Testament. Jesus said that everything expounded on him in the law of Moses (the initial five books of the Old Testament), "the prophets and the songs must be fulfilled." This implies our Old Testament is packed with pictures and predictions of Christ.

Christians can't stand to disregard the Old Testament; it is the preview of the New Testament. Here we see that Jesus was cautious by his own words to show these predictions himself.

These people were well-grounded in the Old Testament; they retained and contemplated it, but they missed some crucial focuses. Jesus reminded the Jerusalem Council later on, "For from early ages Moses has had in each city the people who preach him, for he is read every sabbath in the synagogues" (Acts 15:21).

The people knew Moses, but they missed the predictions about Christ. Not one of those predictions would go unfulfilled. The suggestion here is that had the disciples comprehended the predictions, they would not have been so stupified before the risen Christ. "Everything ...must be fulfilled" included even Christ's triumph over death and the grave.

There is a note of reprimand (rebuke) in Christ's words. He had taught them faithfully while he was with them, before his execution, now he must show them again God's great plan for man's redemption. The disciples were floundering tragically and despair, since they couldn't see how redemption could come through an executed Messiah.

So frequently Christians miss God's blessing in light of the fact that they prejudge what God can and can't do. They maintain a strategic distance from decision openings since they figure God can't do anything through and with them.

They too easily acknowledge rout and get used to discovering some other reason throughout everyday life. Faith calls for wisdom to what God says, despite the fact that the way appears to be impossible.

Jesus Opened Their Minds
(v. 45)

Jesus not only convinced the disciples of his physical reality, he also opened their minds to catch the spiritual realities revealed in Scripture. This is the critical step that was vital before they could get their commission from him.

Jesus calmed their fears and questions; they likewise required scholarly understanding (intellectual understanding) and assurance. They needed to understand everything the Old Testament said about Jesus. This was significant for their mission to their kindred Jews. They must have to demonstrate that Jesus was the Messiah foretold in the Old Testament.

In Acts, when the gospel was preached the Jews, perpetually each point was substantiated by reference to Old Testament prophecies. The mission of taking the gospel must be established in (rooted in) scriptural certainties. The gospel isn't a man-made plan; it was revealed by God.

The proclamation of the gospel must be supported or backed by the authority of Scripture.

To be a compelling servant (to be effective) of Jesus Christ, one must comprehend the Bible. For this situation, Jesus himself did the teaching and opened their minds. Today, the Holy Scripture teaches Christians as they study Jesus Christ's words in the Bible.

It is conceivable, obviously, to read and not get it. Many people know a sprinkling of Bible actualities (facts), but they are not converted. Each Sunday a huge number of people hear Bible teaching and preaching, but they don't understand it. The explanation is that they have not yielded to Jesus Christ's lordship, they are not walking under the influence (control) of the Holy Spirit.

(What was the condition of the disciples right now? What steps are required if one is to learn and understand about Jesus Christ in the Bible? For what reason is this knowledge and understanding essential to carrying out Jesus Christ's Great Commission?)

Jesus Told The Disciples What To Do
(Luke 24:46-49 KJV)

Jesus proved his reality to that small gathering of scared disciples, explained the Scriptures to them, and afterward gave them a particular task. What a mind-extending task it was, to preach in the name of Jesus Christ to all countries. That task, or commission, has never been rescinded.

Faithful believers have accepted and believed it as God's will for their lives. Several them have died for Jesus Christ in completing this commission. Without obedience to this task, there would be no churches in America today.

We owe our spiritual wealth to the individuals who first took the gospel westbound. Today there are a great many people who are yet to hear this sublime (glorious) message.

Jesus Had To Die And Rise
From The Dead
(v. 46)

Here is the sum and substance of the prophetic message about Christ. "It is written" doesn't allude to a particular verse, but to the overall thrust of the prophets. This, obviously, is the thing that

Jesus himself had instructed. These were the two vital focuses about Messiah that the disciples couldn't accept, however without these two there is no gospel.

The death and resurrection of Jesus establish the heart of what Christians need to tell the world. The first missionaries, Barnabas and Paul, focused their message on these realities (Acts 13:26-37).

The gospel isn't simply one more strict custom, not simply one more arrangement of rules. The gospel focuses to explicit events in history that can be checked. Christians welcome people to consider and contemplate what befell Jesus Christ, why he suffered, and why he rose from the dead, alive once again.

These noteworthy certainties make Christianity extraordinary. They have stood the trial of insightful investigation. At the point when people have explored them, they have discovered more than history; they have discovered the significance of life for themselves. The gospel is noted ever, however it changes people the way in which no other fact of history can.

During that time people have attempted to isolate supposed Christian values from Christ's death and resurrection. The cross and the unfilled tomb have been made light of and the morals of Christ's ethical lessons have been underlined.

In any case, there is no genuine Christianity without Christ's death and resurrection. He had to experience the ill effects of the dead, or there would be no forgiveness to offer people. He had to die and rise again in view of the holy law of God.

God's holiness required judgment for sin and sinners; his justice necessitated that the punishment, which was death. That is the reason the gospel is "Christ dying for our sins." He didn't die to be a legend or a saint, however to take the just sentence that every individual deserved, in light of the fact that "all have sinned and fall short of the glory of God" (Rom. 3:23).

Jesus likewise had to rise from the dead, or his death would not have gained victory over transgression (sin). He rose to demonstrate that he defeated sin and death; he rose again with the goal that anyone may know him personally.

You can know Jesus today because he is alive; you can't know any human that way. The resurrection was final evidence that we can be forgiven and set free from both sin's punishment and power.

Repentance And Forgiveness Must Be Preached In All The World
(v. 47)

Jesus Christ's death and resurrection are of no use, except if people repent. Nobody can be forgiven except if he repents. In this way, the commission of Christ advises Christians to preach repentance and forgiveness.

The instruction given by Jesus here was completed exactly by Peter. He originally gave the realities of late history and afterward he called for repentance (Acts 3:19). This is the example for us today. Knowing the realities of Christ's death and resurrection won't save a person except if he/ or she repents.

These realities are expected to deliver a change in heart and mind; that is the thing that repentance is. The person who repents alters his perspective on God, about transgression (sin), and about oneself. He/She acknowledges the way that he (or she) has abused God's laws, that he (or she) has trespassed (sinned), and that he/she is destined to eternal punishment except if the person in question is forgiven.

The person likewise alters his perspective on Christ. Christ is never again an odd figure of history, however a living Savior who can be welcomed into one's life. Along these lines, forgiveness is a difference as a primary concern that prompts a difference throughout everyday life. That an individual can be forgiven is uplifting news (good news) surely, yet it is uplifting news only if an individual understands that the person should be forgiven by God. This feeling of need becomes out of considering God to be holy and oneself as a sinner. Except if one is forgiven, there is no expectation of salvation and everlasting life.

To be forgiven implies that God never again considers you responsible for your transgressions (sins); the punishment of judgment is expelled; God takes a look at you as righteous in Jesus Christ.

Here, at that point, are the significant parts of the Christian's message. It is a message that must be preached in Jesus Christ's name to all countries. Preaching here just means proclaiming.

It might be done officially in a customary community gathering, or it might be done casually in one's home or in a discussion at work or over some espresso. One thing is sure: it isn't restricted to expertly prepared individuals (professionals).

Truth be told, the commission (Great Commission) was given to every one of the believers gathered there in Jerusalem. The followers started to preach on Pentecost, however, soon the good news was taken to Antioch and somewhere else by Philip and numerous other people who were not disciples.

No Christian is prohibited from Jesus Christ's commission. You may need understanding and preparing, but if you know Jesus Christ as your Savior, he has a particular mission you to perform.

Throughout the entire life of the church, this example was followed. The church was planted first in Jerusalem, but then under the missionary Paul and others inside a couple of decades churches had been established all through the Roman realm. "All countries" (or all nations) signifies truly all people in the earth.

We are not restricted by national limits. A few nations today are shut to evangelist work, however the people can be reached by Christian radio, (and TV in some cases)broadcasts and correspondence courses.

The church needs full-time missionaries to make the most of the many chances to preach in Jesus Christ's name today. Many clans and tribes are reachable that were not reachable previously. New techniques for mass correspondences are accessible. Today, as at no other time, God has given the church many energizing chances to obey Jesus Christ's command.

The Christians Were Witnesses
(v. 48)

Jesus helped the early believers to remember what they had seen, to be specific his death and resurrection. Since they were witnesses, they would occupy an exceptional place throughout the entire existence of the church.

In any case, any person who has experienced the truth of Jesus Christ in their life by faith can be a witness. A witness essentially tells what he/ or she has experienced. This is a good way for any Christian today to be a "witness" in his very own backyard, so to speak.

The Holy Spirit Would Empower Them
(v. 49)

"The promise of my Father" alludes to the coming Holy Spirit (John 14:16, 17, 26; 16:7-11). Jesus reaffirmed that he would complete his previous promise to them. In the mean time, they were to hold up in Jerusalem until they were "clothed with power from on high" (cf. Acts 2). This is an excellent picture of what God accomplishes for Christians who pay attention to Christ's command seriously.

These early believers were fearful; they weren't searching for new worlds to overcome; they would not like to preach Christ anyplace, let alone to all countries. Be that as it may, Jesus Christ gave them a message and a command; at that point he gave them spiritual power.

Any faithful Christian can confide in God for the strength to do his will. God doesn't expect anybody to accomplish more than God himself empowers him to do. Each believer receives the Holy Spirit when he confides in Jesus Christ, and the indwelling Spirit provides direction and guidance for each progression of obedience to Christ's commission. The church grew at that point and it keeps on growing now on the grounds that the same Holy Spirit is at work.

(How would you have felt after hearing these words, had you been one of these disciples? What obstacles and fears would occur to you? What opportunities? What would be an important factor in deciding to obey Jesus? What keeps Christians from taking this Great Commission more seriously?)

The Believers Worshiped With Joy
(Luke 24:50-53 KJV)

This is a lovely picture. Jesus went with this frightful band outside Jerusalem to Bethany and there he blessed them, knowing very well indeed how they felt. However, his teaching, his commission, and his blessing changed them.

They returned to Jerusalem, the hotbed of resistance to Jesus, and worshiped ceaselessly in the sanctuary (temple). Now they were filled with praise and joy in light of the fact that the risen Christ had vanquished their fears. At the point when we enable him to do that for us, we will show the sort of happiness - even in hard places - that will be a witness to Christ and his love and power.

Conclusion: Jesus Christ has a plan, a commission for each Christian. The devastated Christian attempts to maintain a strategic distance from 100% obedience to that plan; the rich Christian euphorically surrenders his very own plans and grasps Christ's, despite the fact that it might take him (or her) to unimaginable lengths with the gospel. There is no choicer privilege in this life.

Bibliography

The Holy Bible (1964) Authorized King James Version. Chicago, Ill.: J. G. Ferguson

The Holy Bible (1982) New International Version. Grand Rapids, MI.: Thomas Nelson (Used By Permission)

The Holy Bible (1978) New York, NY.: New York International Bible Society (Used By Permission)

The Holy Bible (1953) The Revised Standard Version. Nashville, TN.: Thomas Nelson & Sons (Used By Permission)

The Holy Bible (1901) The American Standard Version. Nashville, TN.: Thomas Nelson (Used By Permission)

The Holy Bible (1959) The Berkeley Version. Grand Rapids, MI.: Zondervan (Used By Permission)

The Holy Bible (1977) The New American Standard Bible. USA.: The Lockman Foundation (Used By Permission)

The New Testament In The Language Of The People (1937, 1949) Chicago, Ill.: Charles B. Williams, Bruce Humphries, Inc, The Moody Bible Institute (Used By Permission)

The New Testament In Modern English (1958) New York, NY.: J. B. Phillips, Macmillan (Used By Permission)

The Wycliff Bible Commentary (1962, 1968) Nashville, TN.: Chicago, Ill.: The Southwestern Company, The Moody Bible Institute Of Chicago

Barclay, W. (2001) The Gospel Of Luke (The New Daily Study Bible) Louisville, KY.: Westminster John Knox Press, St. Andrews Press

Gideon, V. E. (1967) Luke, A Study Guide. Grand Rapids, MI.: Zondervan Publishing House (Used By Permission)

Gutzke, G. M. (1975) The Go Gospel: A Discussion Guide To the Book Of Mark. Grand Rapids, Mi.: Baker Book House (Used By Permission)

Gutzke, G. M. (1977) Plain Talk On Mark. Grand Rapids, MI.: Nashville, TN.: Zondervan Publishing House (Used By Permission)

Gutzke, G. M. (1966) Plain Talk On Luke. Grand Rapids, MI.: Zondervan Publishing House (Used By Permission)

Lane, W. L. (1974) The Gospel According To Mark: The English Text With Introduction, Exposition, And Notes (The New International Commentary On The New Testament) 2nd Edition. Grand Rapids, MI.: Cambridge, UK.: William b. Eerdmans Publishing Company (Used By Permission)

Wolf, E. (1900) An Exposition Of The Gospels. Philadelphia, PA.: Lutheran Publication Society

About The Author

THE REVEREND DR. JOHN Thomas Wylie is one who has dedicated his life to the work of God's Service, the service of others; and being a powerful witness for the Gospel of Our Lord and Savior Jesus Christ. Dr. Wylie was called into the Gospel Ministry June 1979, whereby in that same year he entered The American Baptist College of the American Baptist Theological Seminary, Nashville, Tennessee.

As a young Seminarian, he read every book available to him that would help him better his understanding of God as well as God's plan of Salvation and the Christian Faith. He made a commitment as a promising student that he would inspire others as God inspires him. He understood early in his ministry that we live in times where people question not only who God is; but whether miracles are real, whether or not man can make a change, and who the enemy is or if the enemy truly exists.

Dr. Wylie carried out his commitment to God, which has been one of excellence which led to his earning his Bachelors of Arts in Bible/Theology/Pastoral Studies. Faithful and obedient to the call of God, he continued to matriculate in his studies earning his Masters of Ministry from Emmanuel Bible College, Nashville, Tennessee & Emmanuel Bible College, Rossville, Georgia. Still, inspired to please the Lord and do that which is well – pleasing in the Lord's sight, Dr. Wylie recently on March 2006, completed his Masters of Education degree with a concentration in Instructional Technology earned at The American Intercontinental University, Holloman Estates, Illinois. Dr. Wylie also previous to this, earned his Education Specialist Degree from Jones International University, Centennial, Colorado and his Doctorate of Theology from The Holy Trinity College and Seminary, St. Petersburg, Florida.

Dr. Wylie has served in the capacity of pastor at two congregations in Middle Tennessee and Southern Tennessee, as well as served as an Evangelistic Preacher, Teacher, Chaplain, Christian Educator, and finally a published author, writer of many great inspirational Christian Publications such as his first publication:

"Only One God: Who Is He?" – published *August 2002 via formally 1st books library (which is now AuthorHouse Book Publishers located in Bloomington, Indiana & Milton Keynes, United Kingdom)* which caught the attention of The Atlanta Journal Constitution Newspaper.

Dr. Wylie is happily married to Angel G. Wylie, a retired Dekalb Elementary School teacher who loves to work with the very young children and who always encourages her husband to move forward in the Name of Jesus Christ. They have Four children, 11 grand-children and one great-grandson all of whom they are very proud. Both Dr. Wylie and Angela Wylie serve as members of the Salem Baptist Church, located in Lilburn, Georgia, where the Reverend Dr. Richard B. Haynes is Senior pastor.

Dr. Wylie has stated of his wife: "she knows the charm and beauty of sincerity, goodness, and purity through Jesus Christ. Yes, she is a Christian and realizes the true meaning of loveliness as the reflection as her life of holy living gives new meaning, hope, and purpose to that of her husband, her children, others may say of her, "Behold the handmaiden of the Lord." A Servant of Jesus Christ!

Printed in the United States
By Bookmasters